THE
ST ANDREWS
of JO GRIMOND

The author standing outside his birthplace in Abbotsford Crescent

THE
ST ANDREWS
of JO GRIMOND

ALAN SUTTON

First published in the United Kingdom in 1992 by
Alan Sutton Publishing Ltd · Phoenix Mill · Far Thrupp · Stroud
Gloucestershire

First published in the United States of America in 1993 by
Alan Sutton Publishing Inc · Wolfeboro Falls · NH 03896–0848

British Library Cataloguing in Publication Data

Grimond, Jo
    St. Andrews of Jo Grimond
    I. Title
    941.292

ISBN 0-7509-0207-8

Library of Congress Cataloging in Publication Data applied for

Typeset in Bembo 11/14pt.
Typesetting and origination by
Alan Sutton Publishing Limited.
Printed in Great Britain by
The Bath Press, Avon

Contents

Acknowledgements

In writing this volume I have used books, people, my memories and my eyes. I have not read all the histories and guidebooks dealing with St Andrews, nor have I attempted to cover in any detail the more celebrated buildings in the city or the events concerned with them. Readers who wish to find out more about the history of St Andrews will find that it has been covered by many historians more expert than myself. The St Andrews Preservation Trust has published an admirable series of pamphlets on the city.

I would, however, like to record how much I have enjoyed and benefited from: the First and Second Statistical Accounts of 1793 and 1838; Andrew Lang's *St Andrews*; Professor Read's *Historic St Andrews and its University*; and Dr Ronald Cant's *The University of St Andrews*. I must also particularly mention *Building for a New Age*, edited by Dr John Frew. There may be other cities which have been the subject of architectural guides as good as this one, but I do not know of them. Dr Hay Fleming's *Guide to St Andrews* would be a pleasure to read even if you never visit the city. Its advertisements evoke all the life and bustle of an age before supermarkets and motorcars.

Pre-eminent among those with whom I have talked are Mr Robert Smart and Dr Cant. The former, who is Keeper of the Muniments at the University of St Andrews, is marvellously informative about St Andrews, and if anything is lacking in his knowledge Dr Cant will supply it. I must thank them both for the trouble they have taken in reading and correcting my often inaccurate memories.

I must also thank several other old friends for their help and their comments: some have also provided photographs and stories. Among them are: Mr Edward Lee and his half-sister the Revd Marie-Louise Moffett; Mrs Pamela McNeile; Mrs Helen Prain; and Mrs Jean Tynte. Mr D. Hotchkiss kindly supplied remarks on his uncle and Mr Andrew McIntosh Patrick helped in finding illustrations. My nephew, Mr Mark Black, has unearthed various articles and photographs and plied me with excellent hospitality. I am indebted to Mrs Reid, who was a Kyle of the golfing family, for reminiscences of the Austin and Sloan families. The letters of Sir Edward Playfair have given me a new pleasure in life. Among my sources of information are back copies of the *Fife Herald* for which I am indebted to Mrs Winifred McNamara. Mrs McNamara has been most kind in not only supplying information but getting it copied. I must also thank the Bursar of St Leonard's School for her help.

I must formally thank those who have allowed me to quote from works whose copyright they own. I am grateful to Mr Adam Fergusson for allowing me to quote from George Dempster's *Letters to Sir A. Fergusson*, edited by Sir James Fergusson, to Dr John Frew for permission to quote from *Building for a New Age*, to Messrs Faber & Faber for permission to quote from *The Selected Letters of Somerville and Ross*, edited by Clifford Lewis, to Mrs Wilson for quotations from her article on Sir Hugh Playfair's garden in the St Leonard's School gazette, and to Lord Bonham Carter for a quotation from his mother's letters.

I would also like to thank David Buxton of Alan Sutton Publishing for making the production of this book such a pleasurable experience.

As often before I must thank Miss Catherine Fisher, MBE for

valiantly coping with my handwriting.

I must thank Mrs Helen Prain for the photographs of the Children's Putting Links, Roger and Joyce Wethered, Francis Ouimet, Jesse Sweetser and Cyril Tolley. Mrs Pamela McNeile supplied the photographs of Dr Paton and his son, John and my nephew Robert Corbett provided those of my sister Gwyn and Ian Collins. I am grateful to them as I am to the St Andrews University Library Photographic Collection for permission to reproduce pictures taken from their collection. Many of the other photographs come from the *Fife News Almanac*, which holds a fascinating record of Fife affairs, and I am grateful to the *Fife Herald* for allowing me to use them. I thank Mr Jim Henderson of Aboyne who took some of the photographs.

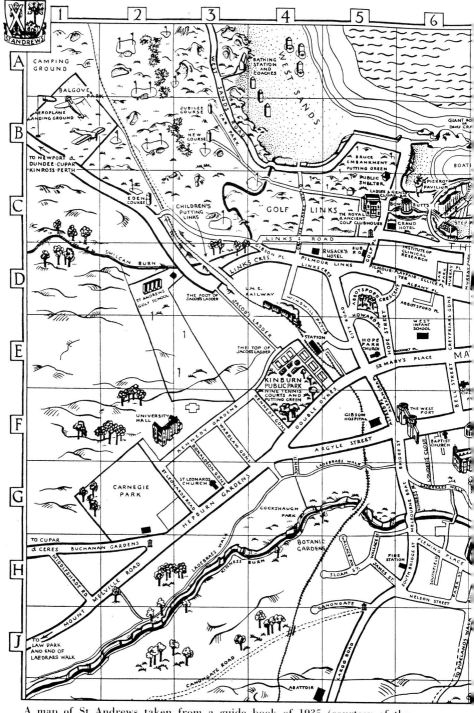

A map of St Andrews taken from a guide book of 1935 (courtesy of the St Andrews Merchants' Association)

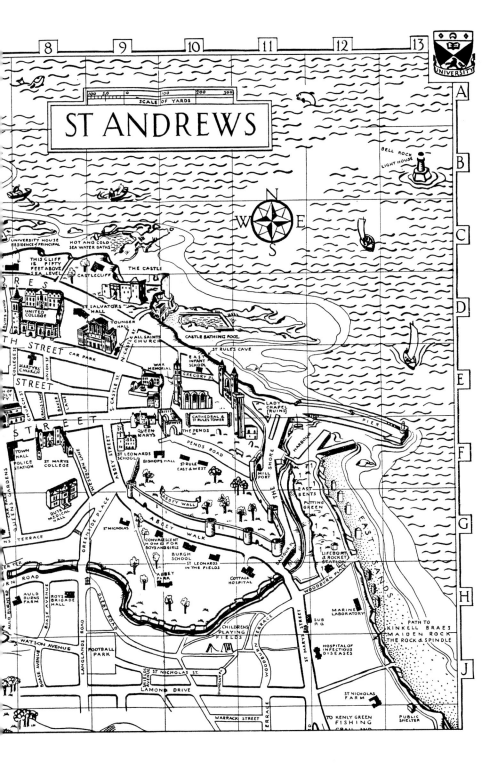

Introduction

S t Andrews is a famous city: famous not only for golf, that Royal and Ancient game played for hundreds of years by the many and the great, but also as the Canterbury and Oxford, or the Rome and Bologna of Scotland: the home of its metropolitan see and oldest university. It is a great European and, indeed, world city visited by thousands of people from America and Asia.

Despite its fame the St Andrews that I remember and the St Andrews that I still like to visit is a clutter of people and buildings. However well known throughout the world, it was to its inhabitants, and especially to their children, a world of its own which belonged to them. That is how I see it. In my childhood the foremen porters were more real to me than the prime minister or Prior Hepburn. So, the reader should not expect this book to give them a history of the city. Anyone wanting help with the thesis for their doctorate on St Andrews would be well advised to keep clear of it. It is not very accurate, concise or well-balanced. But I hope that it may persuade a few people to tear themselves away from the golf courses and the West Sands and take a walk or two through its streets. Perhaps when they have read all they can stomach of Cardinal Beaton and Knox, and even of great golfers and have seen enough of ruins – even the most splendid – they may like to look at St Andrews as a town which has lived for a long time and sheltered all sorts of people, many of whom, in spite of the toll of martyrs and murderers who are featured so prominently in the history books, lived happy lives.

It is a satisfactory size for a town. You can walk easily from one end of it to the other – and that is what I recommend you do. Magnificent as its ruins are, it also has a range of good houses dating from the sixteenth century to the present day. Many of its small houses have now been repaired and repainted, thanks in some measure at least to the St Andrews Preservation Trust.

The countryside and the sea run into St Andrews. The farms which still held cattle in my boyhood have vanished, but the shore and the Ladebraes are full of birds and from the houses in the main street you look out onto the fields of Fife.

I have divided the town into walks but, of course, no one will follow such walks exactly. I do not want to encourage too much trespassing, but much of the best in St Andrews is to be found round odd corners and down small wynds (lanes). I hope as you wander round, this guide will help you see into the houses of some of the people who once lived there and to imagine the wonderful variety of shops which at one time graced the city.

Golf and its Surroundings

The prow of St Andrews, the point at which the town juts out into the countryside on the west, used to be that pile of houses in a modified Scots baronial style which forms the corner where Gibson Place meets the Links. Standing there today you can see two of the most out of place buildings in Britain. On your right, as you face north, you will see a large building in the nineteenth-century Station Hotel style peculiarly inappropriate both in size and colour – being six or seven storeys high and red. It used to be the Grand Hotel, now taken over by the university and called Hamilton House. The best that can be said for it is that it is not badly proportioned and has an endearing vulgarity. The Grand Hotel was a convenient land-mark for caddies pointing out the line to golfers coming up to the last few holes. One poorish player irritated his caddy by constantly asking for 'the line'. Each time he got the same laconic answer, 'Just play on the Grand Hotel'. On going out again in the afternoon he said jocularly to the same caddy, 'At least you can't tell me now to play on the Grand Hotel'. 'Na, na,' the caddy replied, 'just keep your arse on it.'

Not even these excuses are open on the second horror, the St Andrews Old Course Hotel, another hotel which sits ugly, graceless and out of scale to your left. This nondescript building

3

has wrecked the landscape. St Andrews railway station once stood on this site; in my boyhood it was only the goods station, the passenger station having been moved into the town. Not a thing of beauty perhaps, but to small boys a joy for ever. It was also famous to golfers from all over the world, bearing as it did on its black sheds the name of Anderson, renowned makers of golf clubs, over whose 'A' intrepid drivers from the seventeenth tee trusted their balls to carry over a segment of the station, and vanish from sight to re-appear triumphant on the fairway.

Before it was built the Old Course stretched unsullied to the Eden; now its four innermost holes have been enclosed and suburbanized. Perhaps the Royal and Ancient Golf Club, which makes considerable profits from golfers keen to play its famous courses, will start a fund to pull the hotel down.

Looking for lost golf balls in the whins was a healthy and respected trade for caddies out of employment. Repaints were a cheap resource, especially for children. One man, however, showing enterprise before the days of Mrs Thatcher, hid in the old station, popping out from his lair to capture his prey of balls before their owners could round the sheds. It shows how high both golf and honesty were esteemed that when he was caught the police traced who had been playing that day and called on them to allow them to claim their golf balls that evening.

It seems strange now to remember how abrupt was the end of the city of St Andrews. Coal carts certainly went in plenty to and from the old station. Across the road from the seventeenth green, between the road and the railway embankment, lay the children's putting links, the scene of constant competitions for which small but genuine silver cups were presented. Going to the competitions was an expedition often accompanied by a picnic tea. The bumpy fairways of the putting green were cut from 'the rough'. The whole, though only fifty yards from the Athol Hydro Hotel, was a small rural world of its own.

1   Golf at St Andrews according to Sir Francis Grant, PRSA

2   Putting on the Ladies' Putting Green, 1920

3   Charles Tolley (left), amateur champion in 1920 and 1929, and Captain of the Royal and Ancient in 1948, with Jesse Sweetser (right), amateur champion in 1926

4   Francis Ouimet, member of the winning team of the US Walker Cup in 1922 and Captain of the Royal and Ancient in 1951

5   Roger Wethered was the amateur champion in 1923, and he only lost the Open Championship in 1921 because he trod on his ball. He was Captain of the Royal and Ancient in 1946

6   Dean of Guild Linskill (right) holding young Tom Morris' putter, seated next to Fred Mackenzie (left), with whom he played an annual putting match on the Ladies' Putting Green

8   Alison Hopwood

7   Joyce Wethered (Roger's sister), one of the finest women golfers who won the women's championship in 1922 and 1929

9   The Children's Putting Green competition for the Cox Cup, 1922. Helen Skene is in white at the back, and I am the boy with the sticking-out ears near the front

10   Provost Norman Boase driving himself in as the Captain of the Royal and
Ancient. Originally a competition was held and the winner declared captain

11   From left to right: Gordon Lockhart, professional at Gleneagles; Willie
Auchterlonie, Open champion in 1893 and professional at the Royal and
Ancient; R.T. Jones, amateur champion 1926–7 and 1930, and Open champion
1927 and 1930. In 1930 he won four British and American championships.
Norman Boase is far left

12 The Prince of Wales and Lord Castlerosse on the first tee of the Old Course

13 Ian Collins and the author's sister Gwyn during the Scottish Hard Court Championships, *c.* 1930

14 Jimmy Alexander, the starter, greeting Will Fyffe, who does not appear to be prepared for golf

16 'Kate Kennedy' on the arm of Professor McIntosh, 1929. Professor McIntosh is in the uniform of a captain in the St Andrews University Artillery Volunteers

15 The 'Kate Kennedy' pageant in 1932. 'Kate' (G.A. Graham) is escorted by Professor D'Arcy Thompson and her uncle, 'Bishop Kennedy' (Q. White).

17 Principal Sir James Irvine with Stanley Baldwin, General Smuts and Sir J.M. Barrie striding out purposefully to instal Smuts as Rector in 1934

Looking down the Swilcan burn from this point where Gibson Place meets the Links you will see an extremely agreeable little humped bridge made of sandstone. It was not, as I was brought up to believe, built by the Romans but it has been there for a long time, first appearing in seventeenth-century prints. According to the First Statistical Account, during the eighteenth century there were only three bridges in the parish of St Andrews which extended about 10 miles by 4 miles. Two of these were over the Kinness or Ladebraes burn. The third, presumably the one we are looking at, was on the road to Dundee. However, it must only have been used by pack-horses and all trace of a road has disappeared. Presumably the Swilcan, which is rather a miserable, though historic, burn was normally crossed by a ford. Mr Burnet, the historian of the Royal and Ancient, thinks that the bridge was probably used principally by fish merchants taking fish from St Andrews harbour to Cupar. The original road seems to have run further south so that it is doubtful whether 'the golfers' bridge' was used by pedestrians or pack-horses. The roadway, which gives its name to the seventeenth hole (the road hole), later became a turnpike or toll road in about 1800. The bridge may therefore have always been intended for the use of golfers.

Walking along the Links towards the eighteenth hole you pass a jolly, white house with bow windows and a balcony. This was the home of the Shields, who were not particularly notable, but Mr Shields painted when not making linen in Perth – and painters have been strangely rare in St Andrews. You then pass the New Golf Club, second only to the Royal and Ancient as a home for golfers. In fifty yards or so you cross the mouth of The Wynd where that street debouches from the main road to cross the golf course. Here you can read a notice which, though no doubt proper and legal, slightly raises my hackles. It advises you rather peremptorily to go round the eighteenth green and first tee rather than cross the course. It also informs you that golfers have priority. Indeed? The land from the Scores, at least as far east as where the Catholic church now stands, right out to the Elysian Fields and skirting on to the Eden, was common land, the property of the burghers of St Andrews. Golf was tolerated. In my time the families of all ratepayers played free and the Cheapes of Strathtyrum were accorded certain privileges such as playing off on the Old Course whenever they chose. 'Zanda' Cheape, the owner of Strathtyrum, once caused consternation in the Royal and Ancient Club by remarking that he would find it very conven-ient to take sand and shells for his farm from Hell Bunker – which he claimed to own.

In summer a happy band of holiday-makers streamed across the course bound for the West Sands: horsemen and women, parents, prams, cyclists and children with buckets and spades, rather like those friezes of pilgrims on their way to Canterbury which illustrate Chaucer. The official name of this road is, I believe, Granny Clark's Wynd. I never heard it referred to as anything but The Wynd. My grandmother lived in the only house in it but I remember nothing of her or her home. Her daughter, however, was a princess among aunts; one of those essential features of family life, she shed balm and local news among us Grimonds.

Resisting the temptation to defy the notice and cross the golf course we continue on beside the eighteenth hole up to the town. Rusacks Marine Hotel, which was the most fashionable hotel in St Andrews, is on our right; over the years the world's best golfers must have stayed there. I wonder where its registers are? The Rusacks were a family of German origin, and being an old established St Andrews family did not save them from coming under suspicion as spies during the First World War – it having been suggested that Mr Rusack, a most loyal, respected

and elderly man, had signalled to German submarines from the
roof of his hotel.

Passing Rusacks and the home of the Kyle family, several of
whom were good golfers in their day, we reach the Ladies' Golf
Club, St Rules. (Rule is a synonym for Regulus, the saint who
brought the bones of St Andrew ashore.) St Rules was for St
Andrews ladies what the Royal and Ancient was for men. Its
clubhouse, as you can see, is not so imposing as that of the
Royal and Ancient but it too has its bow window looking out
on the course, and it too enforced a certain decorum. A row,
famous in its time, broke out when my sister and her sister-in-
law gave a tea for a black professional in the club. You may not
now be able to recapture the feelings aroused, but seventy years
ago the battle lines were firmly drawn between those who felt
that to be male, professional and black were three reasons each
in themselves enough to ban their possessor from the club. In
the other camp were those who held that hospitality, skill at
golf, good looks and origin within the Commonwealth over-
rode all other considerations.

Next is the site of the house of Hugh Philp of revered
memory among golfers – the inventor of that snake-headed
wooden putter so elegant to look at and so treacherous to use –
now Tom Morris's shop. This shop is named after the Morris
father and son who between them won the Open Championship six times. It has, however, had no connection with their
family for a long time – certainly before my time. You then
come to what is now a shop selling woollen jerseys, etc., the
only variety of shop except those dealing in electrical goods,
mortgages or 'gifts' which seem able to compete with supermarkets. This used to be Forgans. Forgans and D. & W.
Auchterlonie were perhaps *primi inter pares* of the five club-
makers of the 1920s. In those days all clubs had hickory shafts.
Drivers, brassies (with a brass plate on the bottom) and spoons

7

or baffies could be bought ready-made, but most were made by hand to the measurements of the purchaser. The cost as far as I can remember was about 15s. to £1 each. The hickory shafts for irons, cleeks, driving irons, mid irons, lofting irons, mashies, jiggers, mashie-niblicks and niblicks were also handmade. But the heads were bought in from cleek-makers. One of the best known in St Andrews was Stewarts, whose trademark was a pipe and whose forge was off Argyle Street.

Mason's Golf Hotel once stood on the corner of the Links and Golf Place. Between it and the Royal and Ancient the caddies mustered. In the little pavilion a ballot was held in summer for starting times, the result being pinned up each evening. The fountain is a memorial to Provost Playfair designed by Lorimer. Where the Grand Hotel, now transformed in to the university's Hamilton Hall, stands was the site of the Union Club Parlour in the old days, the clubhouse of the Union Club, a fairly humble one-storey building. The Union Club was the first St Andrews golf club, the forerunner of the Royal and Ancient. The notion of a clubhouse seems to have come from the association of golfers with the Society of Archers, revived in 1834. The Archers provided a room for golfers and it was this room that was first known as the Union Club Parlour.

The land which you are now looking at stretched past the Elysian Fields to the Eden, and comprised the Old, New and Jubilee golf-courses and the sandhills down to the sea. Originally, as I have said, they belonged to the burgh of St Andrews. The burgh from time-to-time sold or leased parts of it, usually reserving some rights for the citizens. There is a long record of those tortuous transactions so beloved of lawyers but frequently the cause of disputes. The main causes of friction were golf and rabbits. As early as 1552 John Hamilton, Archbishop of St Andrews, who built the facade of the present castle and helped to establish St Mary's College (a doubtful character, however, who was eventually hanged for complicity in the murder of the Earl of Moray), received a licence from the Town Council for making 'cunnigairs' or rabbit warrens on the links, but under the reservation of the community's right to play golf, football, etc. In the early years of the nineteenth century a famous case involving the Dempsters, who had bought part of the links subject to various reservations, went by way of numerous interlocutors, appeals and interdicts all the way to the House of Lords, only to be sent back after twelve years to the Court of Session where it was only ended, according to Lord Moncrieff, because the rabbits came to an end. So the golfers won. As well as rabbits various rights to take turf must also have interfered with golf. In my youth it was assumed that the town owned the Old Course. Hence, it was the right of all ratepayers and their families to play free, though the Royal and Ancient paid for the upkeep of the course. On weekdays, with due care for golfers, the public were free to walk on the fairways and indeed dry their linen upon the whins, while on Sundays no golf was played, and all could walk as they pleased.

The Royal and Ancient was founded in 1754, when the Union Club already existed, but it had no premises until the middle of the nineteenth century. Its members were largely concerned with arranging competitions, drawing up the rules of golf, defending the rights of golfers and eating and drinking at various taverns. The two clubs were not exclusive. On the contrary, most members belonged to both. In 1852, as the Union Club parlour was small and in need of repairs, it was agreed to amalgamate the clubs and build a new clubhouse across the road. The Town Council agreed to feu (lease) the land for a guinea a year. Two of the oldest caddies swore that the ground had never formed part of the golf-course so no golfer could object. Mr Rae was appointed architect and

Mr Whyte-Melville laid the foundation stone. The building of 1854, as it stands today, has been considerably altered and extended especially in 1880–2 by John Milne, while its big window was added by Mr Foggo of Perth in 1877. But the basic form and design derives from Rae's original plan.

The Royal and Ancient clubhouse is full in the summer and during competitions, but in the winter it is under-used. During the day it makes a salubrious club for locals with excellent lunches. But the last time I went there on a winter's evening my host and I were the only occupants besides the staff. There are plenty of staff because of the profits from the championships it organizes although it does give away most of the takings for the good of golf. Traditionally it has had close links not only with the town of St Andrews but with the county of Fife. The Royal and Ancient held its dinners and balls in the town hall and among its principal members were many Fife lairds – indeed its captaincy used to be shared alternately by a well-known member from far away and a Fifer. Fife, at least up to the Second World War, produced enough good golfers to keep its end up, Colonel Skene, of an old Fife family of which we shall hear more later, being typical as a scratch player and a Fife laird.

Up to the Second World War the Royal and Ancient served as a general club. Many professors, businessmen and other residents went down in the evening, as some still do, to drink, read the papers and gossip whether they played golf or not. Indeed it was said, libellously no doubt, that one professor of a previous generation, having at his inaugural lecture found the lecture room unbearably cold, adjourned to his house and never again in winter ventured out except to visit the club. As some professors at one time did little or no lecturing in the summer, his life must have been reasonably comfortable. One reason why I suspect the club is less used in winter and in the evening is because of the departmentalism of modern life. Instead of using a club in common with general citizens of St Andrews, the university has its own staff club where its staff will see and meet only others from the university. This is one of the curses of modern life. Everyone is segregated according to the organization to which they belong, leading to in-grown and bureaucratic habits. I remember with pleasure a young market-gardener in a London club telling a Lord Chancellor what nonsense he was talking. Had he been a lawyer in a club for lawyers only, he never would have dared.

The centre of the clubhouse is the Big Room looking over the Old Course. It also has excellent billiard tables where I have spent many a pleasant evening with John Paton, son of the doctor of St Leonard's School. What it did not have were elaborate changing rooms: golfers played in their ordinary clothes, plus-fours being deemed normal dress in St Andrews. Naturally, the clubhouse contains many mementos such as the Victoria Jubilee Vase and the Calcutta Cup, also medals and the club on which each captain hangs a medal. Portraits of ex-captains are on the walls of the Big Room including an excellent one of the Prince of Wales, later Edward VIII, by Orpen showing him with his eyes shaded by his cap, a favourite trick of the artist's. While staying at Rusacks the prince made an impression by wearing a Fair Isle pullover and even more so by getting up early to practice the bagpipes. He is wearing the pullover in the portrait. But you will notice, if you are lucky enough to see the portrait, that he wears no jacket. Yet if you look at the photographs of contemporary golf champions you will find that most played in tweed coats.

The captain plays himself into office each year on the morning of the Autumn Medal Day. He presented the caddy who retrieved his ball with a gold sovereign. It was an ordeal made worse for poor golfers, a category which included several famous, indeed royal captains, by being hemmed in by a ring of caddies who were judges of form and, guessing that he would not drive as far as the road, jostled in an intimidating pack as near as a hundred yards from their new captain. The ordeal was crowned by the firing of a cannon when he reached the top of his swing.

In 1860 we are told that 'an extraordinary tempest raged on the medal day', the wind from the north was howling and the rain lashing. Just as the parties were about to start, a cry was heard that a vessel was being wrecked in the offing. Play for the medal was postponed. The lifeboat was launched but there was great difficulty in getting it manned. Maitland Dougall, who was about to play when he heard of the difficulty, volunteered to go and took the stroke oar. The men were rescued and the lifeboat came ashore in the afternoon. The play for the medal was begun after the arrival of the lifeboat. The wind was still furious. It was to Maitland Dougall's credit that, though his arms were still sore and he was stiff and wet, he took the club gold medal at 112 strokes.

Beside the Royal and Ancient clubhouse a flight of stone steps leads down to the golf-course – forming a small grandstand for the finale of championships and a triumphal way for the victor. If from the top of these steps you look west, you will see beyond the stone bridge over the Swilcan the tee for the eighteenth hole. It looks a long way away and indeed it is, some 350 to 400 yards. Yet Ted Blackwell in the days when golf balls flew with less agility than now and with a wooden-shafted club bounced his drive off these steps.

Ted was one of the Blackwell brothers, the most notable amateur golfing family of their day, or perhaps of any day. The Blackwells were men of rugged build and craggy face, like ancient trees hardened by St Andrews gales. They were not much given to emotional outbursts – nor indeed small talk. As his brother, Walter, having holed a tricky putt to win a foursome competition, started to pick his ball from the hole, all Ted remarked was, 'I think that is my ball Walter.' It is also said that when Walter was travelling by train in the USA, a stranger in his compartment looking out of the window when they stopped at a station remarked, 'Say, isn't that quite something, this station is called Blackwell and so am I.' On being asked what he said in response to this double coincidence, Walter replied, 'Oh I didn't say anything.' The oldest brother, Jim, had given up golf by the time I knew them and looked after the links.

Now, going down some steps you reach the first tee over which presided 'Alexander the starter'. His was a most responsible job. No doubt he had to resist many efforts to bribe him by golfers who had not won a starting time in the ballot. His office was a sentry-box. As he was rather fat he filled it, even though he had lost one arm. From the window of this cabin his voice carried over the heads of the assembled golfers and cabbies announcing not only which golfers were to start next but who was caddying for them. He was no respecter of rank. When the turn of the ex-prime minister (a poor golfer) was reached he announced, 'Mr Macgregor [a celebrated caddy] is carrying for Balfour.' He was very nice to all boys and girls and himself played golf in spite of the loss of his arm.

Leaving the club behind us we go down a footpath between the fairway to the first hole and the Bruce embankment, which was once occupied by two putting greens, one a few pence more expensive to use than the other. Stuck in the sand off the Bruce embankment at the mouth of the Swilcan burn was all that remained of the good ship *Princess Wilhelmina*, presumably her forepost. It has now gone. To the west stretch the sands. In my childhood striped bathing-boxes were pulled into the sea by horses. Occasional treats, such as donkey rides, were to be had and once aeroplane rides from Sir Alan Cobham's flying circus, which took the reputedly oldest man in the world up for a flip.

After landing and being asked the usual journalist's question, 'What did you think of it?', he gave the excellent reply, 'Much the most exciting thing since news of the battle of Waterloo.' He must have been coached.

Passing down the north side of the first and second holes, leaving the Bruce embankment on the right, we take the path to the New Course which is leased to the Royal and Ancient, although again in my youth it was free to ratepayers and their families. On the way you cross what used to be the Ladies Putting Green, a most entertaining putting links comprising small alps. An important event in the golfing season was a competition on this links for prizes presented by the new captain of the Royal and Ancient. Very elegant some of them were. I possess a silver tea caddy won by my mother. The putting green had its difficulties. The farmer, a Cheape, who also claimed ownership of the land, is said at one time to have insisted that the holes be filled up each evening. A road has now been laid between the Old and New Courses, one of the gestures no doubt to the large and lucrative crowds which follow championships and such like. It might be much worse. I did not see any cars on it. But the whins have been somewhat scarified, so the scene seems to me like some bearded veteran with a fine head of hair who has suffered a crew cut. And there are rakes in the bunkers; thus the fashions of America and suburbia march on. I met a man on a motorbike dressed like a member of the crew of an oil rig with 'Ranger' emblazoned on his crash helmet. What must Mr Lees, the ranger of my time in his tweed cap, or indeed what must old Jim Blackwell who ran the course for the Royal and Ancient and patrolled it in a mackintosh, think of their successor? Every week they tramped many miles over the courses. Today's changes include a thing like a naval target, no doubt a grandstand, erected by the Eden estuary. I hope that it is taken down in winter.

Golf has become solemn as befits big business. At St Andrews it has long been a serious matter, but in my youth neither so ponderous nor so expensive. For players to take much more than $2\frac{1}{2}$ hours to go round the course was to risk ostracism from decent golfing society. My mother, a brisk and good golfer, estimated 2 hours 20 minutes as sufficient and ruthlessly enforced the right to play through the match in front if they fell more than a hole behind, even if it was a four-ball composed of venerable members of the Royal and Ancient. Though players concentrated on their shot they forewent the extraordinary preparation now common. Nearly everyone nowadays takes a practice swing before each shot and engages in prolonged meditation upon each putt, sometimes prostrate on the green. Incidentally, I learnt in my golfing days to be wary of any opponent who, instead of the hunched and unhappy stance common to putters, strode up to his ball, stood four-square to it and as though driving knocked it self-confidently into the hole. In putting, as in other things, it is confidence which counts. As for the expense, I am baffled by the cost of everything today – even allowing for inflation. The links were immaculately kept in the past, the greens like billiard tables, yet the cost seems to have been a fraction of today's. It cannot be because they are used more. There is only the same amount of daylight (floodlighting, thankfully, has not yet been introduced) and they were full all summer. One cause of extra expense is the abominable habit of taking a divot with every iron shot, a habit made more common by the substitution of the niblick and high trajectory shot for the jigger and run-up.

With the many millions of pounds made from golf spectators you would think that the course would welcome, free-of-charge, locals of all ages and skills as St Andrews did in my youth. Today golf, the democratic game, at least in Scotland, has become a rich man's sport. The poor boy or girl has little chance of knocking a ball about on a good course unless he or she has the skill to be exploited by the bureaucracy and paid for by the taxpayer. It is the usual story: first we make something too expensive and then it is subsidized. On winter evenings in my youth I could take a few clubs and practice on the second or seventeenth holes.

As for the implements of the game, they have, of course, grown in numbers and expense. Seven or eight clubs carried in a canvas bag used to satisfy good golfers. Now an arsenal is towed around in a portmanteau. We happen to know the cost of clubs and golf balls in the past from the diary, written by the early seventeenth century, of no less than the Marquis of Montrose. The price of golf balls seems, not surprisingly, to have varied. Two 'golfs', or golf balls, at one time cost 10s. and at another 24s. A drink before and after golf cost 45s. 4d. James Pett was Montrose's club-maker and 'for sax new clubs and dressing some auld clubs and four balls' he was paid '£1' (1 Scots pound) 8s. James Pett also made bows and arrows for Montrose, and Pett's daughter nursed Montrose while he was ill, supplying him with chickens, jelly, sack and sugar possets. Pett's accounts also include: 'To the poor and boys who carried my Lord's clubs that week – 8s.'

However, to return to modern times. The only fault which can be counted against St Andrews – unless you think too many 'blind' approaches a fault – is that it is lacking in holes requiring a medium to long iron for a good golfer on a calm day. Holes around 480–500 yards in length. This could easily be rectified. You only have to add about 150 yards to the ninth and tenth holes. This could be done without spoiling the character of the holes. You could re-create the somewhat featureless ninth green and approach further north by cutting back the whins. A pity perhaps to cut more whins, but let some of the others grow up. Otherwise the only change would be the removal of that symbol of our civilization, a public lavatory. In bygone days the place of this judiciously concealed 'convenience' was taken by a ginger beer seller who provided refreshment at the tenth tee. He might be resurrected.

A walk to the Eden used to be worth taking even if you did not play golf. Between the Old Course and the sea lay the New Course and the Jubilee or Duffers' Links. As I learnt to play on it I had an affection for the last. No bunkers, no fearsome carries, indeed few whins and not much difference between the greens and the fairways. The New Course was all right but uninspired. The whole region out by the Eden estuary was wild, and lit up by the yellow of the whins and the daisies, heather and wild flowers. The air seemed to be particularly translucent, dancing in the breeze and full of the song of larks. The sandhills seemed like the Himalayas. There used to be a shooting range, so remote was the area at the end of the sandhills. Hay Fleming recalls that a party of farm servants were gathering seaweed when one of them was shot through the foot. The farmer confronted the officer in command of the range and after expatiating on the injury received by the man ended up by exclaiming, 'An' man, ye ken, it micht hae been a horse.' Now the Duffers' Links have been 'improved', the sandhills seem to be lower; a dreich road stretches to the Eden and tourism has gripped in its dead hand what used to be a paradise, if a humble one.

On the other side of the Old Course lay the Eden Course. This seemed rather remote as its first tee lay behind the old station which entailed a considerable walk before you could begin to play golf, and the first two holes were cut off by the railway. But I liked the course, it had some interesting holes and if we could not get off on the Old most of my generation preferred to play there rather than on the New.

The game played on the Old Course at St Andrews is

different from golf as played on the heavy inland soil of most golf-courses. It does not depend on 'traps' to catch the ill-hit shot. It is to my mind a superior and a much more subtle game. But like so many masterpieces of an earlier age which depended upon faith and a good eye (medieval cathedrals for instance) it may sink under too much popularity. 'We all kill the thing we love.' Just as the feet, breath and motors of the tourists are destroying Notre Dame in Paris, so too many golfers may ruin St Andrews.

The difficulties that the city faces are not confined to the suburbanization of the links, they arise also from the flood of motor traffic. However many golf courses you make near St Andrews the pilgrim-tourists will want to visit 'the Old'. But the start of the Old Course is not so much a bottle-neck as a bottle. Once you get half a dozen buses and a score or two of cars in Golf Place behind the eighteenth green, the parking is full up and access or egress blocked. Nor is there any other space to exploit. Even in winter, South Street, Market Street, North Street and the Scores are full. The sand dunes, once a wild terrain for children and birds, are now pathetically dwindling between erosion and traffic. A vile ribbon of tarmac stretches behind them and kiosks demand payment at their entrance.

Unless the tourist trade evaporates – which the shops would not like – I can see no answer. You could, I suppose, build an underground car park north of the Scores, with an entrance by tunnel, but even the revenues of the Royal and Ancient would wilt before the cost. You cannot build out to sea for fear of increasing the erosion which may, in time, threaten Prior Hepburn's walls. Perhaps you could make tourists park outside the town. But as the human race becomes less and less keen to walk, you would need a fleet of buses to shuttle backwards and forwards to the golf-courses. The solution may be to stop trying to devise ingenious schemes which, if successful, may only succeed in increasing the traffic, and let the streets silt up until movement becomes impossible. Then we should rebuild the railway.

Another peculiarity of St Andrews arises from the separation of the ownership of the golf-courses from the clubhouses. None of the St Andrews golf clubs own a golf-course. The Royal and Ancient clubhouse naturally only admits its own members. It does not get the green fees, nor bear any responsibility for the visitors who play on the courses. The town provides no pavilion or clubhouse. Unless, therefore, the visitor is staying in a nearby hotel, his or her changing room must be their car. And since nowadays people no longer stroll down to the links in their work-a-day clothes but put on shoes with fearsome spikes and jerseys with fearsome colours, changing is a necessity. As another feature of St Andrews is a shortage of hotel space in the summer months, despite the new hotel and all the guest-houses, the visitor may be unable to dress as he or she thinks appropriate within a quarter of a mile of the course.

The Scores
and the Sea

We start the next day at the back of the Royal and Ancient. Here we are at the headquarters of the game which for hundreds of years has meant so much to the town. We tramped the links yesterday; we are now to explore the habitat of countless golfers, visitors and residents. Lord Cockburn, author of that splendid book *Memorials of His Time*, stayed at the Black Bull in 1844, which was then the name of Glass's Tavern in South Street, for many years the senior hotel of the town. He noted that:

the natives have a pleasure of their own, which is as much the staple of the place as old colleges and churches. This is golfing, which is here not a mere pastime but a business and a passion and has for ages been so, probably owing to their admirable links. This pursuit actually draws many a middle-aged gentleman whose stomach requires exercise and purse cheap pleasure to reside here with his family. There is a pretty large set who do nothing else, who begin in the morning and stop only for dinner. Their meetings are very numerous and they are rather a 'guttling' population.

The same was true of the St Andrews of my youth. Mr

Boothby who stayed in the house which my family subsequently rented, 8 Abbotsford Crescent, was a notable golfer who was famous for the songs he sang accompanied by his son, Bob, later an MP. One of these ran:

We've been gowfin a' the day and done nae work at a'
Rinnin' aboot wi' a bag of clubs a chasin' a wee white ba'
A cloutin' it aff the tee a shoutin' our o' 'Fore',
Rinnin aboot wi' a bag of clubs a chasin' a wee white ba'.

From the Royal and Ancient we climb the Scores. Why Scores? Dr Cant states that it comes from a Nordic word meaning cliff. Anyway, the houses look west and north over the cliffs, a good view at all times so long as you do not take in the new hotel. The view is particularly fine at sunset when, as de la Mare wrote in celebration of his honorary degree at St Andrews, 'The rose of Eve beams far and wide.' On the way up from the Grand Hotel you pass a house which used to be Le Maitre's School. Mr Le Maitre, the headmaster, had two children who were first-class classicists: Sir Alfred who, after being wounded in the First World War, rose to high rank in the Admiralty; and Ella, who became a prominent school teacher in both Britain and South Africa. Another daughter, Barbara, operated a system of signals from her window to that of Geoffrey Curran in Abbotsford Crescent, which we will reach in due course. The Asquiths later rented the house during the holidays when H.H. Asquith was Member for East Fife, although St Andrews was not in the constituency, it being one of the Fife burghs. Scotland went on having groups of towns linked together and separated from their rural hinterlands until after the Second World War. It was rather a sensible arrangement for, in some cases, the burghers had little in common with the counties. A letter from Asquith's daughter, Violet, tells of the hazards of electioneering in 1904:

'After four meetings we were motoring to our last at about 10.30 on a pitch dark road in a strange car. We drove full tilt into the curb stone. There was a crash, a lurch, the wheel came off, the car went right over on its side and then partially recovered itself. The motor was very heavy and entirely covered with glass. Beyond a bad jar and shake we were neither of us in the least hurt. We had to drive twenty miles, found the other meeting still waiting for us in the middle of the night and reached St Andrews in the early morning.'

The Asquiths, Herbert and Margot, were keen but poor golfers.

In an attempt to promote St Andrews as a medical centre between the wars, the Mackenzie Institute was set up in a neighbouring house. But St Andrews has too harsh a climate to nurture the infirm. If you are not killed off by the east wind before fifty, you have a fair chance of lasting into your eighties unaided by clinics. As the Second Statistical Account states, 'the situation of the city is particularly salubrious but in April and May the east wind generally predominates. It is then . . . peculiarly piercing and chilly and is regarded as injurious to persons of a delicate constitution.' This did not kill the British passion for bathing.

The rise in the popularity of St Andrews as a resort coincided with the enthusiasm for sea bathing which swept the middle and upper classes of urban Britain during the nineteenth century. (I do not believe that the craze caught on among countrymen or manual labourers; I have noticed that native Orcadians are far too sensible to risk immersion in Scottish waters.) Despite temperatures more suited to seals than humans, my friends and I bathed almost daily in summer. So it is no wonder that Mr Hay Fleming's guide gives advice on swimming:

> The water is attractive but nervousness prevents persons learning to swim. No one should be forced. Avoid bathing within two hours of a meal or when fatigued or cooled after perspiration. Wet the head on entering: and when treading the water is learned try the stroke. Leave the water when there is a feeling of chill, and emit water through the nostrils. Watch you never bathe from a boat not anchored. A good swimmer might experiment in a dip with clothes on.

Rather gruesomely, Hay Fleming then instructs the merry tourist on how to behave if he or she is drowning. There are also hints on artificial respiration and the restoration of the half-drowned.

Beyond the bathing place, long seaweed-covered rocks slide out to sea, breaking the top of the tides like stranded whales, and at low tide indented by pools and encrusted by barnacles. Slithering out on these rocks you could watch rafts of Scoter and Scaup ducks bobbing up and down behind the waves. These flocks may have diminished but not, I think, disappeared, and there are eiderduck, mergansers and many varieties of gull also to be seen.

The shore is worth exploring from the mouth of the Eden all the way round to St Andrews harbour. I used to bicycle out along the sands, my great grandfather's ten-bore gun strapped to the crossbar of the bicycle. And very cold it was, hard pedalling against the wind. But if it was a warm, still morning, then there was little hope of a shot. Bags were indeed small. In ten years I shot one pink-footed goose and a brace of widgeon.

St Andrews is renowned for its sunsets, but it is worth

getting up to see the sunrise over the bay and strike the church towers. A really bad frost brought snipe and mallard to the mud-flats nearer Guardbridge and, all through the winter, flocks of waders whirled and glided along the shore. I was never much good at identifying them, but out with Doris Wilson, whose family house we shall pass, I seem to remember seeing over fifty species of birds in and round the city. At one time mussels were gathered round the Eden estuary to be sent away mainly for bait.

Going on along the Scores the open land towards the sea was part of the same common land which included the golf-courses. It was called the Bow Butts as archery was practised on it. The martyrs of the Presbyterian church who suffered during the Reformation, particularly Wishart, are commemorated by a rather good monument built in 1842 and designed by Nixon. The unfortunate old women burnt on this land as witches are not commemorated.

Number 3 the Scores was the home of Jim Blackwell and his family, young Jim and Lorna. Young Jim was a fine golfer in the Blackwell tradition. Edith, Lady Playfair, one of the clan Playfair who figured prominently in the history of the town in the nineteenth century, lived in the white house with round windows. The widow of Lord Playfair was a Bostonian described by her great nephew Giles Playfair as 'an American lady of incredible dignity and severity . . . who when in London drove round Hyde Park every day in a carriage-and-pair'. The Playfairs are a prime example of that group of families who through many generations distinguished them-selves in the clerical, academic and professional life of Scotland and the public life of Britain. Many of them pursued careers in the Empire, particularly India. The change to self-government in the colonies and dominions closed what was a rewarding outlet for many sons and daughters who looked to wider fields than their small country could offer.

The first member of the family to be prominent in St Andrews was the Revd James Playfair, Principal of the United College of St Salvator and St Leonard. He was arraigned before the local church court at the instigation of his rival principal George Hill, of whom Playfair's counsel, Cockburn, wrote 'George Hill [was] the most graceful and externally elegant but the meanest of political priests. I never abused any man with such cordiality as I did him for about four years.' From Principal Playfair the Playfairs seem to have inherited not only great talents in friendship as well as learning, but a streak of paternalism. One of his sons was Hugh Lyon Playfair, most prominent of St Andrews' provosts, whose house we shall pass on a later walk. Lord Playfair, the scientist, was his grandson. He was an archetypal Victorian of the finest vintage. He was educated at St Andrews, Professor of Chemistry at Edinburgh University, MP, friend of the Prince Consort and Mr Gladstone's Postmaster General. He was also involved in numerous projects and commissions, invented the postcard, suggested the Victoria and Albert Museum and wrote such a savage attack on the drains of Buckingham Palace that it had to be suppressed. 'A great sewer ran through the courtyard and the whole palace was untrapped . . . I painted a small room in the basement with white and it was blackened next morning.' Lord Playfair's photograph shows the square head and slightly protruding eyes typical of some Playfairs. While he is given the expression of concern and even severity thought appropriate, you can detect in the photograph that enjoyment of life and humour which similar features more obviously displayed in his nephew Sir Nigel Playfair the actor-manager, who invented special trousers for hikers which could be attached to their shorts and so render them 'properly' dressed when entering hotels. Indeed, like many Victorians, Lord Playfair was a man of greater liveliness and eccentricity than most members of the modern establishment. As Special Commissioner for the Great Exhibition of 1851, when the bishops objected to naked statues among the exhibits, he suggested that they should lend their aprons. He was attending a banquet in Paris when some soldiers broke into the marquee to steal the food. Playfair appears to have joined them looting a chicken and a bottle of champagne – both of which, however, he was forced to give back. Later in this house lived the present Lord Harris of High Cross, one of the first presiding spirits of the Institute of Economic Affairs which played a leading part in the repulse of socialism in the 1970s. He was a lecturer at the university.

For a time Mr Macfie, the first amateur golf champion (1885), also lived on the Scores. He was a lightly built, spry old man with a pale complexion, a sharp eye and he held his head tilted to one side. He was very deaf. He also lived in the district of Rathelpie at one time. It was said that when he was a bronco buster in Australia his mates had put a burr under his saddle, the horse had bucked and thrown him and he had been deaf ever since, – an unlikely story. Anyway, deaf he was and cussed. He seems to have been an early exponent of gamesmanship. According to Sir Guy Campbell, when several holes down he remarked that he did not think Sir Guy was driving as far as usual. Sir Guy pressed. Macfie won. He was a friend of my mother's. She was also deaf. He used to roar rude remarks at her in the street, to which she responded in kind. They never met without this 'flyting'.

Mr Inglis, who ran Steel Coulson, the Edinburgh brewers, lived in The Hirsel. Before you reach Murray Park there are three houses, Craigmount, Kilrule and New Halls, which have been altered and two of them joined. In them lived notable St Andrews families of the inter-war period. One was the Austin family. Captain Austin was secretary of St Leonard's School. The Austin family let their house in the summer and took to their tents. One of their children, John Austin, became a respected philosopher of the most advanced and unintelligible sort. He was a Fellow of Magdalen. The other family was that of the minister of the Hope Park Church, Dr Sloan. He was also for a time provost of the city and the provost's lamps stood resplendent before his house. I regret that local authorities, in spite of delighting in squandering money, have abolished such lamps. However, the lamps have found a permanent home outside the town hall. Dr Sloan paid a visit to South Africa and long afterwards his sermons had an African tinge.

Passing the south of Murray Park, now entirely given over to bed and breakfast guest-houses, on the right you should notice a rather charming cottage designed by Henry. Its neighbour must have been one of the first houses built outside the confines of the old city. Opposite is the Roman Catholic church, a modest but good building; the first of Reginald Fairlie's numerous churches. The marble East End is not his. Only four saints are commemorated in its windows, one of which is St Magnus of Orkney. The priest tells me that Magnus was given refuge by a Pictish king then ruling in Fife. This confirms my view that the Picts were rather nicer than the Scots. My belief is that all the major upheavals in Britain were mistakes. How much better it would have been if the English had defeated the beastly Normans at Hastings; if the Reformation had taken a different turn and if the Stuarts had retained their throne.

Next on the left are several improbable and large houses. The first, designed by Hall and Henry, was inhabited by two well-known St Andrews families, the Jacksons and Dalmahoys. Then comes what was the residence of the principal and vice-chancellor – in my day Sir James Irvine – University House, designed by Edinburgh architect, Starforth. Sir James was a forerunner of the modern generation of vice-chancellors. The standards and standing of the university had been raised by his predecessor, Donaldson. To enable it to maintain and improve its position, Irvine saw that it must find more funds and publicize its attractions. With this in view he spent much time travelling and taking part in activities outside the university. He remained, however, a respected local figure with a popular family. His only son, Nigel, was sadly killed in the Second World War. Sir James was a noted expert on sugar, who persuaded Harkness to give his large benefactions, one of which we shall soon reach. But pause to consider the changed life of the bourgeoisie to which leading academics belonged. The Irvines had a ten- or twelve-bedroomed house, three, four, perhaps five servants, but no grand car that I remember, certainly not one supplied by the university. In the latter days they had a country cottage – but only I think in the very latter days and perhaps only after Sir James died, when it became their home.

Moving along, you pass two truly extraordinary houses linked together, Edgecliffe, designed by Rae who built the Royal and Ancient and, as we shall see, several modest and semi-classical terraced houses. The St Andrews architects were versatile. Edgecliffe is one of the wilder fantasies of the Scottish baronial style. This style, peculiar to Scotland, is a strange affair. In its original form it only became fashionable when gunpowder was rendering castles obsolete. Having, like Gothic, been more or less eclipsed during the eighteenth century it erupted in the nineteenth. Supposedly well matched to the craggy, mountainous landscape of the Highlands, it became a badge of success for wealthy town dwellers. I expect these towers could be explained by Veblen as a gesture by the rich to show how little they need be concerned with utility – as with the wearing of the top hat. But their towers and crow-steps, corbelling and spire-capped pepper pots are very strange.

The eastern half of the building, of which Edgecliffe is the west, was lived in by a man with the resounding title of the Revd Sir Nicholas Beaton Bell. Professor Rose occupied the west half after leaving South Street. Professor Rose bathed in the sea almost every day, appropriately perhaps as his wife was a daughter of Plimsoll, of Plimsoll-line fame. The next house, no mean structure, in the same style was inhabited by a well-known St Andrean, the Revd Dr A.K. Boyd. It was afterwards thought suitable as a rectory for a none-too-rich Episcopalian minister.

Opposite the principal's house on the south side of the Scores there was once a boys' school, and behind it gardens belonging to the university containing a fine sycamore and bush roses. The courts or yards of Scottish universities differ not only in layout but in atmosphere from those of Oxford or Cambridge, as though they were designed for walking rather than sitting, which in the climate of Scotland is sensible. The back view of the buildings in Butts Wynd, which bounds the east end of the garden, and the buildings in North Street are particularly agreeable. The building in the middle, the 'new' University Library, is not so agreeable, being in the lumpish, all-purpose style. Should the university ever be closed it will serve equally well as open-plan offices. Professors and lecturers, no doubt, have all sorts of gadgets, word processors and computers, but their offices do not seem to have been designed as rooms for human beings. In the parking area you may note a curious notice: 'Warning Exhaust Fumes'. In such an office you will find Mr Smart, keeper of the Muniments for the University. He not only knows the history of St Andrews, but is constantly adding to our knowledge and spreads his knowledge with a generosity which would do credit to Bishop Kennedy himself.

The buildings on whose backs I have commented favourably were renovated by Sir Robert Rowan Anderson, who also designed the Swallowgate at the Scores end of Butts Wynd. The Wynd itself leading from the old town to the Bow Butts we shall leave until tomorrow. Opposite the junction of Butts Wynd with the Scores a road leads down to the sea, now the entrance to a private house. In my day it led to the Ladies' Bathing Place. The house was occupied, at least in summer, by the Spens family, well-known Glasgow lawyers. Then on the sea side comes Castlecliffe, built in 1809 by Bryce, one of the best-known exponents of a style derived from Scottish baronial but modified to turreted Victorian. Castlecliffe is a big house in large grounds and has inevitably come to be owned by the university. It is not my favourite house, nor is Bryce my favourite architect.

Opposite Castlecliffe on the south side of the road stands the first men's hostel built with money given by Harkness. It was designed by Mills, who lived in St Andrews, although his office was in Dundee. His home was in North Street between St Salvator's College and the Younger Hall. It seems to have disappeared. His son, Ken, was a fiery socialist in his youth. He made a memorable speech at the Oxford Union after which the student paper, aping a then common advertisement, commented, 'Nature in the raw is seldom mild'. In later life he became a successful businessman. Not very appropriate to the city, being in 'universities' Cotswold style, the building is rather successful though the site is cramped; at least it is as good as Nuffield College, Oxford. The colleges of St Andrews University, St Salvator's, St Leonard's and St Mary's, were originally residential. It was only fairly late on in her history when the poverty of the university, rather than inclination on the part of the colleges, led to the amalgamation of St Salvator's with St Leonard's, while St Mary's became confined to theology, that the tradition of Scottish students being treated as independent adults grew up. East of St Salvator's Hall on the Scores stand two large houses, one of which was lived in by General Grogan and his family and another by the Riddell-Websters, one of whom was Quartermaster-General in the Second World War. Some seventy-three years ago you might have found me, in a rebellious mood, being drawn in pastels by Mrs Maitland Ramsay, wife of an oculist, in the drawing-room of one of these houses. I have the picture still.

Further east are the ruins of the castle between the road and the sea. The accounts of the death of Wishart (commemorated on the Martyr's Memorial), the murder of Cardinal Beaton (or Bethune), the siege, and other such events and the bottle dungeon are in many books and guidebooks. Happier events in my time took place in the house opposite – Castlemount, the home of the Paton family. Castlemount was one of the most sensible and comfortable St Andrews houses as it was without a basement or pinnacles and only two storeys high. Dr Paton, who qualified at the age of twenty-one, was the doctor of St Leonard's School, a genial Scots doctor of the old school who drove an Arrol-Johnston car which suited him very well, it being spacious and, as cars went in those days, reliable. Earlier, I am told, he puffed about St Andrews in a steam-car. He was universally popular, having the ability of all good doctors to sympathize with his patients and arouse affection in response. Our own doctor, MacTier, was also sympathetic, but he horrified my mother who once found him and my aunt, who was in bed, puffing away at cigarettes which were forbidden to her. MacTier explained without shame that to be deprived of tobacco caused her too much unhappiness. Dr Paton was reputed to be a brilliant diagnostician. He tried out all the new medical samples sent to him on his wife, Maisie, who was a Boase, a sister of Philip and Norman whose houses we pass later. She was a capable and friendly woman. In spite of their business abilities the Boases had an unworldly streak, innocent or ignorant of much of life. The Patons had three children, all great friends of mine and all well favoured. They were a devoted family but Jock and his son John much enjoyed 'stand-up' rows, during which they did indeed stand up and throw books on the floor. The only redeeming aspect of the tragic fate of the Patons was that John had married Pamela Pollock, a great asset to St Andrews and a solace in the Patons' old age. The two sons were killed in the war and the daughter died of cancer. John, the eldest, was cut out for success, being not only able but congenial and good at games. He did many things well and easily. He was talented and well balanced, good company with what is called an 'open' expression free from arrogance, but not at all defensive. Both the sons, but especially Neil, inherited Dr Paton's sense of humour with its Scottish streak of the 'black'. Of all my St Andrews friends John is the one I miss most.

At the western corner of the Paton's house the Scores proper ends. The direct continuation runs along the top of the cliff, again with marvellous views to the west and north. The turning to the right leads into North Castle Street where we enter the older part of the town, but before going further No. 51 should be noted; built in 1879 for Jesse Hall by himself and Henry, his assistant. Hall, as well as an architect, was the manager of the gas works. Up to the Second World War it was common for one man to perform several jobs both in the public and private sectors. In the 1920s Mr Cantley was not only manager of the gas works but also a solicitor in private practice and the town clerk. This arrangement must have led to considerable economies and worked reasonably well, though there were murmurings that all the council houses were served by gas even though the tenants might have preferred electricity.

Passing Castle Street and going along the cliff, yet another bathing place lies below – this time mixed. Beneath the cliff there is a cave in which, so I was brought up to believe, Lady Buchan gave tea parties. Lady Buchan was the Lady Ottoline Morrell of the St Andrews of her time, entertaining such intellectuals as she could muster. In one of a pair of villas on the right Edwin and Willa Muir lived for a time before moving to Queens Gardens. They claim to have disliked St Andrews, complaining that it was snooty and unwelcoming. I am rather surprised that a man who enjoyed Menton with its 'old-fashioned English colony, its Victorian grace, its superannuated old ladies dressed like Queen Alexandra, its modest incomes and regular habits' should have found little to say in favour of the city and the university. Humphrey Sumner, then Professor of History in Edinburgh and later Warden of All Souls' College, Oxford, who had been my tutor at Balliol, came to stay with us. With the presumption and innocence of youth I assumed that two such distinguished men as he and Muir would be certain to get on well. I therefore hired a wagonette (along with horse-cabs and buses, a common conveyance in St Andrews in those days) and organized a picnic at Kittricks Den along the East Cliffs. Sumner and Muir were shy men. The party was not a success. The Muirs, who seldom got up before midday, were no doubt regarded as too Bohemian for St Andrews' taste.

A little further east we come upon the wall which surrounded the precincts of the priory and of which much remains. When one of the numerous towers which punctuate the wall was being restored in the last century a group of skeletons was found seated in it, giving rise to one of the ghost stories in which St Andrews abounds. It used to be said that if you thrust your hand through a certain crevice in the masonry it would be shaken. An old tank from the First World War was mounted on the bank looking out to sea. I suppose it was thought to be a suitable war memento. It was an object of some interest to boys but it soon became rusted and squalid and was removed, if not pushed over the cliff. Before the war you might have found here a well-known St Andrews lady, apparently enjoying the view and occupied by her knitting. In fact she was keeping her eye on her husband who, advancing into his second childhood, had taken to instructing young girls in sailing.

So we come to where some lines of stones mark all that remains of the church of the Culdees and look down upon the harbour. In the Middle Ages, St Andrews was a considerable harbour. In the days of the Spring Fair it would be crowded with shipping and even in the nineteenth century Dr Smart tells me that it did a fair trade in timber, ironstone and potatoes. Only the last were handled in my youth. Today the most notable feature of the harbour is the pier. I can remember sailing boats (fishing boats?) being warped along it to the basin. On Sunday morning after the service in the University Church the students in scarlet gowns parade on it. It used to be a test of a good head to walk on the rather narrow top of the last section of the pier wall. A ramshackle tenement above the first basin has been renovated or replaced by a dull building. The gas works which, with typical Scots disregard for ancient surroundings, used to rear its chimney between the harbour and the cathedral and lean its ovens over what was once a real tennis court, has been demolished and the surroundings generally tidied up, making it look less like a seaport than ever. But St Andrews retains the echoes and cadences of the sea.

> And the roar of the wind shall refashion,
> And the wind-driven torches recall
> The passing of Time, and the passion
> Of Youth over all
>
> Rudyard Kipling

North Street, the United College and the Cathedral

We start once again at or about Gibson Place. A short deviation down the Cupar and Dundee road as far as the site of the bridge which once carried the railway takes us past John Burnet Hall, a university hostel. It used to be the Athol Hydro Hotel, but I doubt whether enough medicinal water was ever drunk to justify the title 'Hydro'. Sir Steven Runciman, who delivered the Gifford Lectures at St Andrews University, stayed in it. He left his pyjamas behind and his niece, then at St Leonard's School, had to retrieve them. This is the sort of task which would now be set to schoolgirls to test their capacity for drive and initiative – 'Rescue the pyjamas of the greatest of British Byzantine scholars from the hands of the infidel'. Incorporated into the hotel and now the hostel is a house in which Andrew Lang lodged. It was called Alleyne's, presumably after his wife – a Miss Alleyne. Andrew Lang was a student at St Andrews and is the most famous literary character associated with the city, at least in modern times. He, rather sensibly I think, spent the summer in the South and came to St Andrews in the winter, taking various houses but never owning one. *St Andrews by the Northern Sea* is to me a very nostalgic poem. When he wrote 'Like Ocean on a Western Beach the Surge and Thunder of the Odyssey' he must have been thinking of a grey, windy day when the waves break upon the West Sands.

Turning back up to the city you pass Windmill Road on the right: an unobtrusive cul-de-sac, but it was the home of Professor Lindsay, one of the most distinguished of the distinguished professors who taught in the university around the First World War. Professor Lindsay became totally deaf and was, sadly, run over. He was said to be one of the few British Latinists for whom A.E. Housman had much regard. As a student at Balliol I liked the anecdote which tells how, when his nephew, A.D. Lindsay, the Master of Balliol, was staying with him, Professor Lindsay was heard to say to him after lunch, 'Now Sandy run away and amuse yourself, I have work to do.'

The road got its name from the windmill which stood near the passenger station. Some Playfairs also lived in it for a time but it was from Wyvern, just up the hill on the right where the road forks, that the Revd Patrick Playfair, minister of the first charge at the town church, emanated dressed in frock-coat and top hat. Not a man, to use Cecil King's phrase, to whom you would hand your hat, he ruled his congregation with all the God-given authority of a Presbyterian divine and a Playfair. Rather against the will, so it is said, of his Elders, he carried out a drastic repair to the town kirk. Ruthless improvements seem to have characterized the treatment by the Playfairs of any public property in their charge. At the opening of the restored, or rather partially rebuilt, church at a cost which caused

18 Professor W.M. Lindsay, Chair
of Humanity at the university, was
knocked down and killed by a
motorist, at the age of seventy-nine

19 Dame Louisa Lumsden, the first
headmistress of St Leonard's School and
the warden of the first women's hall of
residence

20 All, including the Guard, are engrossed by putting on the sixteenth green
in the 1920s

21 St Mary's garden, St Mary's College

22 St Mary's College – the principal's house and Queen Mary's thorn

23 The tomb of Provost Sir Hugh Lyon Playfair

24 The tomb of Professor Adam Ferguson. It was erected by his children. However, a more imperishable memorial to his genius exists in his philosophical and historical works'

25   St Leonard's School, formerly the home of Provost Sir Hugh Lyon Playfair, and before that the site of St Leonard's College

26   Madras College on the occasion of its centenary

27 Madras College courtyard

28 Edgecliffe

29 Looking north-west from the Scores

30   Houses at the east end of North Street. Number 12 was restored by the St Andrews Preservation Trust and now houses a museum

31   The West Port, 1882

32　Louden's Close　　　　33　Allison's Close

34　The garden side of Queen Mary's House

fidgeting in his congregation, he is said to have remarked, glowering round the crowd, 'There is still £500 owing, a sum I could easily pay myself but I will not deprive you of the privilege' – and he collected it in notes and promises on the spot.

Keeping straight on up the hill past the principal entrance to Rusacks Hotel we pass houses in one of which a member of the MacAndrew family lived – Joe, briefly a Member of Parliament and brother of Charles, Lord MacAndrew. Then comes the shop of D. & W. Auchterlonie, already mentioned. Willie, a former Open Champion, was Professional to the Royal and Ancient and was succeeded in the post by his son. In the shop round the corner in Golf Place, clubs are still made. It bears the name of Tom Auchterlonie but Tom is long dead. His shop used to be beyond Playfair Terrace, to which we shall come. It was next door to Anderson's which had an immense club across the window. Tom Auchterlonie boasted in his advertisement for 1902 a connection with the Japanese Imperial family, so it appears that golf goes back some way in Japan. At the back of Abbotsford Crescent lies Pilmour Place and then Playfair Terrace, designed for the Town Council by Rae and named after the provost.

Across the road there used to be a farm and two nice cottages with tiled roofs. The cattle from the farm were taken in to be milked every day. On this side of the road, just east of where the farm stood, is a turning up into Abbotsford Place, a range of little houses spoilt, as so many houses in St Andrews have been, by the addition of dormer windows. You may notice a car park in which grass has been encouraged to grow between the concrete setts. So what was once taken as a sign of decay has become a symbol of modernism. From here you can look past the end of Hope Street to the rather grander Abbotsford Crescent. On the right still going west, Greyfriars Gardens lead off to the south. Opposite Greyfriars Gardens a piece of 'English Ye Olde Tudor' comes before Murray Park, leading to the Scores with a house by Henry at its western corner, which was the Imperial, once a leading hotel. Notice incised on the wall of the corner house of what is now Greyfriars Gardens the words 'Bell Street'. Originally Bell Street ran all the way from South Street to North Street. Only later was the Monastery of the Greyfriars commemorated in the northern half.

Cockburn who, for all his liberalism, would be considered shockingly 'elitist' today, had a tough attitude to education, especially for the lower classes. 'If St Andrews contributes little to knowledge what college contributes much?' he wrote, and of 'the thing called the Madras College' that it was 'a great blot, there should have been no commonplace, vulgar, bare-legged school here'. He did not care for Dr Bell or Bell Street, 'Which like everything else connected with the founder of the Madras College has an infamonious contemptible new free-stone look'.

After Greyfriars Gardens, North Street is a jumble of small decent houses from the eighteenth and nineteenth centuries. Number 40 was designed by Rae for his own use in 1844. On the opposite side of the road stands the 'new cinema', now St Andrews' only cinema; further along on the right was 'the cinema', now pulled down. It used to be the hub of St Andrews' entertainment. I see in an old advertisement that before the First World War the cheap seats cost 3*d*. for children. Even between the wars they were not expensive. St Andrews owed much to the summer visitors who arrived like a flock of hospitable birds to brighten up August and September. I remember particularly trips to the cinema with some of them. There was another Blackwell family who were no relation to the local Blackwells but something to do with Crosse and Blackwell. They were also good golfers. One of the sons, John, reached the final of the Amateur Championship. Tom, his brother, became a figure on the turf. Their father, Geoffrey Blackwell, seemed a cornucopia of half-crowns to fill the front row of the cinema's balcony with his family's friends.

On the left or north of the street the houses are largely occupied by the university's Fine Art Department. The good building, which used to be St Katherine's School, a preparatory school for girls going to St Leonard,s where a few small boys were admitted, including myself for a very short time, is now the Crawford Art Centre. It was named after that excellent man the 22nd Earl of Crawford and Balcarres who lived not far away at Balcarres and was a most accomplished art critic. Behind it and suitably obscured is the library which we have already passed. Perhaps the most notable artistic possession of the university is its collection of nineteenth-century photographs taken by Cowie and others, including Hill.

St Andrews University deserves credit for not having pulled down old, beautiful, small houses to replace them with modern horrors. It has perpetrated in this century no such atrocity as has Edinburgh, which has destroyed most of George Square and erected the Hume Tower, a bleak abomination in a desert of concrete. But the filling up of the courts behind the street frontages has its dangers. Part of the charm and character of the city lies in delving behind the main streets to find the tranquility of the lawns and gardens behind, as in St Mary's College and Dean's Court.

St Andrews is the oldest of the Scottish universities and far older than any English university with the exception of Oxford and Cambridge. It has had a chequered history admirably set out in Ronald Cant's *History of St Andrews University*. The university was founded by Bishop Wardlaw in 1410 and the college of St Salvator was founded in 1455 by Bishop Kennedy, 'perhaps the only Bishop of St Andrews who has run the risk of incurring the woe pronounced against those of whom all men speak well' as Hay Fleming writes of him. His mother was a daughter of King Robert III. After 1747, when it was amalgamated with St Leonard's College, it became the United College.

Bishop Kennedy is rightly venerated by the university. Every year his 'niece' processes round the town. In spite of girls having been admitted to the university for many years, 'she' is a first year male. The only role for women in the pageant is to soothe the more restive horses, for Kate Kennedy drives in a carriage accompanied by outriders. In the pageant, Scots heroes of all sorts and times are represented, including the great admiral, Andrew Wood of Largo. The principal and professors pay their respects to Kate. You may notice the uniform Professor McIntosh has put on for the occasion. When off duty he was more often dressed for partridge shooting.

Though when the university was founded the only teaching buildings were in South Street, we have reached what were from the early days the main centres of its life – St Salvator's College and its chapel, now the University Church. Some of the university offices are at the head of the Butts Wynd and so, until recently, was the Students' Union in the corner house, which is said to have been lived in by the Admirable Crichton – a celebrated St Andrews student but to me a rather shadowy figure. However, the history of this house, traced by Dr Cant, makes a story of a kind which exists for very few such town buildings in Scotland. Patrick Hamilton was burnt as a heretic outside the entrance tower of the church. His initials are in the cobbles. He is said, on looking up, to have seen Christ's face. It is still there in the stonework. My memory is that when I was a boy it was an elegant Carolean face like Charles I. Now it seems round and rather self-satisfied like a merchant banker. Perhaps it changes with the fashion.

The University Church as seen from North Street seems to

me one of the most beautiful small churches in the world: in the same class – though lower down the scale – as Santa Maria dei Miracoli in Venice. French, English, Scottish, Italian, Spanish and German Gothic all differ from each other. Scottish examples, at St Andrews and Aberdeen, for instance, are rougher and more stocky with whorled tracery. Inside the church is a good pulpit of scrubbed wood and the wreck of Bishop Kennedy's tomb, from which all the silver decoration was picked out by the so-called reformers.

The church forms one side of a quadrangle where once stood the buildings of the medieval college, which were swept away in the nineteenth century. One other side is bounded by the wall of Butts Wynd. Of the two remaining sides the north, and in my opinion the better, is a building by William Nixon (a government architect) which was completed in 1849. The eastern building is by the more famous Robert Reid who designed much of the New Town in Edinburgh. Both are respectable blocks – indeed more than that compared with most modern university buildings – but to me rather uninspired. I cannot help regretting the loss of the buildings they displaced. Had you peeped round Nixon's building before the war you might have found me and Bernard Babington Smith, a lecturer in psychology, playing tennis on a soft grass court on which the game, owing to the lack of bounce, was rather like badminton. Among the few remnants of the old university silver are three maces, among the finest in Britain. (They are illustrated and described in Dr Cant's history of the university.) How they escaped destruction is one of the more pleasant miracles of St Andrews' history.

In my day the students wore long scarlet gowns of wool, lending a beauty and distinction to the city unrivalled by any other university town. The streets were streaked with red against the grey stone. Women students of each year wore a different coloured tassel on their mortar-boards. Divinity students speckled the crowds with black and professors did indeed 'Sail with amply billowing gown enormous through the sacred town.' Professors, however, have never been much good at golf.

The Scottish universities were founded on the continental pattern springing from Bologna and Paris. The word 'university' has sometimes been interpreted as meaning a school or college which taught all knowledge – 'university' standing for universal or embracing all subjects. The medieval phrase for such institutions was, in fact, 'stadium generale'. The universality lay in the fact that universities recruited from far beyond their immediate neighbourhood. Schools were local but universities were world – or at least European – wide. 'Universal' applied to their members not the subjects taught. St Andrews University retains many reminders of its origins. The division of the university into 'Nations' has been abandoned. But first year students are still 'bejants', 'bec-jaunes' or 'yellow bills'. And one of the distinctive features from the past is the office of Rector, originally (as is still the case on the Continent) the chief officer of the university. He was elected by the students and staff; how strange to think that demands of students for some say in ruling the university, a cardinal demand of student revolts in the 1960s, had been realized some five centuries before. The staff naturally objected to being heavily outvoted by fourteen-year-old boys, so in time the Rector was shunted to one side and was elected solely by the students. In the hierarchy of the university he still ranked after chancellor and presided over the court or governing body. He still does – or can. He also appoints a member of the court – probably his most useful function. He has, at least at some of the universities, the right to lecture – a right which struck terror in the professors at Aberdeen when Mr Blackburn, a well-qualified academic and charismatic candidate for the rectorship but of left opinions and editor of *Red Mole* (a paper a lot further to the Left than *Private Eye*), threatened to exercise this right had he been elected. Up to the Second World War the rectors of St Andrews confined their activities to giving a rectorial address. In the nineteenth century many were politicians. By the 1920s the fashion had veered to men distinguished in other fields, such as Nansen and Barrie, who delivered his rectorial on 'courage' which he voted top of the virtues – 'Courage lost, all lost'. One of his chief examples was Bernard Freyberg VC, who received an honorary degree on the occasion of the address.

Crossing over to the south side of North Street, you should look down College Street which leads from opposite Butts Wynd to Market Street. In my youth it housed a 'bespoke' tailor, one or two other little shops and Mr Wisdom the Philosopher (as if he were a Happy Families character). He was the only member of the university who hunted with the Fife hounds dressed in grey flannel trousers. He went on to be a Cambridge professor. College Street has now been polished up and provides desirable residences but, though spick and span, it is unspoilt. Again the Preservation Trust has played its part in the renovations. Further to the east in North Street stands the Martyrs Church, the work of Milne, remodelled by Gillespie Scott. Before the Union of the Churches it was a Free Kirk where my admirable nurse, Jessie Anderson, worshipped. She was, like all the best nurses, a non-conformist. As an example of the standards such nurses set you might ponder on Jessie Anderson's generosity. Although I am sure she never earned more than £50 a year in cash and seldom as much, she educated an orphan out of her savings. He became a professor at Dundee University and his son was Vice-Chancellor of Sussex University. The church is, I believe, admired by connoisseurs as a 'scholarly' example of the Gothic revival. Perhaps remodelling

spoilt it; anyway I do not care much for it. We then come to
Union Street, spoilt by a dull building on the south-west
corner. The rest of the south side of North Street is of good,
plain houses, many with some sober distinction. One, older
than most of its neighbours, has an outdoor stair and one or
two have pantiles.

So we reach the Younger Hall – a magnificent gift to the
university by the Youngers of Mount Melville. I have tried to
like it. It is at least an attempt to produce a work of character and
certainly it houses a fine inner hall. But I must confess that I do
not like it. Its front has no grace or even cohesion. Vaguely
Egyptian in character, it owes nothing to previous St Andrews
architecture, unless the decoration on the top of Playfair Terrace
was inspired by some Egyptian leanings. It is by Waterhouse,
whose father married a Younger. Both here, and indeed in St
Salvator's quadrangle, plate-glass windows lend a lifeless aspect
to buildings which, in the case of the Younger Hall, is otherwise
fussy. The Youngers did not live in St Andrews. Mr James
Younger, who married a Miss Paton (of Paton's wool), lived at
Mount Melville just outside the town. The Youngers were
connected with one of the three Younger breweries; in their case
George Younger beers, which had a 'Y' as a trademark (as
opposed to the little old man with a beard who advertised
William Younger beers). Mr Younger and my father always
played together in the competition for the Autumn Medal of the
Royal and Ancient – they were a serious but not very good pair
of golfers. One of the Younger family, Lord Younger of Leckie,
had been Conservative Chief Whip and another was Lord
Blanesborough, a Lord of Appeal in Ordinary.

On the north side of North Street, before it crosses Castle
Street, I am glad to find a row of holm oaks have been planted.
These trees were a feature of Hope Street but they have been cut
down. Beyond the holm oaks stands All Saints Episcopal

Church, endowed by the Youngers for the fishing community (for whom they also built the Gregory flats, a rather good block looking out over the sea at the foot of Gregory Lane). The church is one of the Waterhouse family's happier buildings. You go in through a little courtyard and surprisingly often find it open. It is dark and very un-Presbyterian but well made with some good stained glass. In my day the rector was the notable Padre Wilson, an Englishman married to a Dane. He seemed to be the epitome of the best type of country parson. St Andrews was lucky that he did not go off to a luxurious living in Norfolk for he was an excellent shot and an ideal shepherd of his flock, as well as cheering up the lives of all who knew him. His step-son, Teddy Lee, is about the only one of my contemporaries from St Andrews that I ever see. His jolly, moon-like face topped by cropped, ginger hair now graces the streets of Henley, looking much as it did in North Street sixty years ago. His two delightful half-sisters still live in St Andrews, one a minister of the Episcopal Kirk. A distinction which she assures me would make her father laugh no end. The padre ended up as Bishop of Moray. Ella, his wife, was a fountain brimming with goodwill and an excellent companion who never lost her Danish accent.

Towards its east end North Street crosses Castle Street, which we shall meet again. Between Castle Street and the cathedral precincts (now occupied by the eastern cemetery) on both sides of the street stand some pleasant houses, once the homes of fishermen, when there were fishermen, and of caddies, their successors. On the south side the St Andrews Preservation Trust own one admirably restored by Gillespie and Scott, that long-serving and notable firm of St Andrews architects who have been building and restoring houses in a variety of styles for more than a hundred years. (Again you should refer to *Building for a New Age*, in particular to the chapter by Mr Andrew Nairn.) This house contains the furnishings of Aikman & Terras the grocers. On the other side of the street lived Mr Whyte, a St Andrews character of the days immediately before the Second World War, in a restored white harled house with curious balcony, rather like a gun emplacement.

Mr Whyte, who appeared in St Andrews rather suddenly, was I believe brought up in America. He was a figure in one of the 'Renaissances' which are recurrent features of Scottish history. The 1930s renaissance was mainly literary though, of course, with political overtones. The East Fife by-election brought Eric Linklater as the Nationalist candidate. I remember him speaking in the Temperance Hall, which was on the site of the 'new cinema', a building otherwise used for sixpenny 'Hops' and sales of work. I expected a romantic hero; I found a stocky figure in plus-fours over whose owl-like face rose an impressive but bald head. I later got to like and admire him. He is under-rated. His writing is easy to read, clear but full of energy: qualities out of fashion in an age which admires turgid obscurity. His book, *Juan in America*, ranks with the best of Evelyn Waugh. Mr Whyte published a short-lived but rather good periodical, *The Modern Scot*, bound in black. He hoped to make his bookshop in South Street a meeting place for St Andrews' lecturers, students and literateurs generally. To some extent he succeeded, but he met with the reserve with which St Andrews greets anything raffish or out of the way. The Second World War put an end to his efforts. Like Mr Rusack, the suspicious St Andreans branded him as a spy. The top of his house does look a little like a fortification, but it is untrue that it was designed as a base from which signals were to be sent to submarines (in any case it faces the wrong way) or as a pillbox from which machine guns would sweep North Street. I remember rather little about Mr Whyte except that he gave me rose-petal jam for tea and appeared free from the vices of which he was accused, being, as far as I could see, neither a traitor, an anarchist nor a show-off.

At the very end of North Street stands the War Memorial designed by Lorimer. Thought by some disappointing, it is certainly not grand nor striking but well proportioned. However, considering its position, it is as well that nothing more striking was attempted – the ruins of the cathedral are striking enough.

The destruction of St Andrews Cathedral, begun in the sixteenth century, was a crime which disgraced the Scots and, in particular, the Presbyterian Church. Started by John Knox, the destruction by neglect and the dismantling of its roof and walls went on long after his death. It must have been one of the more beautiful buildings that the world has seen. It stood on a site unparalleled in Europe. The loss is a tragedy for the Western world and a disaster for Scotland. A bad example of the barbarism which all too often breaks out among my countrymen.

Those who laid out St Andrews, if it was ever deliberately laid out at all, did an excellent and subtle job from which their clumsy successors as town planners could well learn. The town was built along a ridge down which the three principal streets converged on the cathedral. Each led towards the West Front.

The cathedral ruins speak for themselves. Since the history of the building of the great church, its heyday and its degradation have been described by far better scholars than I, so I will pass over any attempt to describe how it must have looked in its full grandeur. It is said to have had a copper roof which shone far out to sea. I find this difficult to believe as the copper would have turned green with verdigris.

Three peculiarities strike me. Embedded in the wall of the cloisters is a smooth, round boulder about the size of a large cannon ball. I presume that it came off the shore. It bears out my view of the roughness of Scottish Gothic. The second feature that I find odd is that the West End is several feet below the street down a steep bank. The conventional explanation is that the ground in front of the West Door is now higher than it was. I have heard this attributed to the dumping of refuse. The Second Statistical Account does, indeed, mention that in the eighteenth century large quantities of rubbish had to be removed from the graveyard. Nevertheless the matter puzzles me. The ground floors of the seventeenth- and eighteenth-century houses to the west of the cathedral are not buried. The 'bank' of rubbish was therefore there when they were built. I can hardly believe that people in the Middle Ages, when the cathedral was a sacred place, dumped enough refuse into its forecourt to make a bank of many square yards in area and several feet in depth. But if the bank is a natural feature, why did they not build the cathedral further east allowing for a piazza in front? Several writers say that the level of the streets near the cathedral have been raised but it would not seem that this alone could explain the considerable drop down to the West Front of the cathedral. The third feature which strikes me as odd is the layout of the site. Several great churches have smaller churches beside them to cater for the needs of the parish, as have York Minster and Westminster Abbey. St Andrews Cathedral had two such satellite buildings, the church and tower of St Regulus and, before its removal to the present site, the town church of the parish. Also, why was the large, heavily decorated gateway set at a right-angle to the cathedral and on a road leading at a tangent to it? Presumably this is because of the priory and the hospital which it maintained for pilgrims; but did the Augustinian monastery, important as it was, overshadow the metropolitan church of Scotland?

The cathedral is now surrounded by a graveyard – indeed the graveyard always came close to its East End. In this part of it the graves go back to the fourteenth century, most of them flat stones on which the lettering is obliterated. I find them moving. But if you are interested in the more recent citizens of the town you should examine the graves round the wall and in the lower plots. You can spend a lot of time so doing and learn a lot about the people of St Andrews. In keeping with his renown the provost, Sir Hugh Lyon Playfair, reposes in one of the more prestigious tombs set into the wall.

Not far away in the same wall lies Adam Ferguson of the eighteenth-century enlightenment, a philosopher and historian of Rome. He was educated at St Andrews and became Professor of Moral Philosophy in Edinburgh. He nearly died when he was forty-nine but eventually lived to be ninety-three by keeping warm and wearing two overcoats. According to Lord Cockburn, 'his gait and air were noble; his gestures slow; his look full of dignity and composed fire. He looked like a philosopher from Lapland.' He neither ate meat nor drank alcohol and only dined out with his relative, Dr Black, when, according to Black's son, 'it was delightful to see the two philosophers rioting over a boiled turnip.' The inscription on his memorial tells us that his imperishable memorial is his philosophical and historical works, 'Where classic elegance, strength of reasoning and clearness of detail secured the applause of the age in which he lived.'

A professor, Fredericus Crombie DD, although he died at the end of the last century, has his inscription in Latin – rather dog Latin I suspect since I can understand it, but Latin nevertheless. He is described as 'Fidelis', 'Eruditis', 'Felix' and 'Dilectus'. Near at hand is a touching little gravestone like the leaf of a book – apparently carved by an amateur, perhaps by a member of the deceased's family. In the corner of the upper graveyard stands the neglected burial place of the Whyte Melvilles.

On going through the gate to the lower graveyard you will find the grave of the Purdie family, around which in spring grow pretty blue flowers whose name I do not know. A custom common in Scotland and elsewhere was to describe a man by his house or lands; it emphasizes his standing and prestige. I like the extension of this designation to be seen on one tombstone which describes the dead man as 'of the Argyle Brewery'. Here lie more Playfairs whose lives are redolent of far-off places and whose distinctions are mainly military. Hugh Playfair of the present generation has provided an exhaustive series of family trees of the family. Another stone marks the grave of 'a golf club-maker' – a description, indeed a distinction, which very few can now claim in the home of golf.

Several Fife families acquired land in Orkney and one of the best known, the Traills, are buried here. They were not universally popular in those Nordic islands. However, one family, the Balfours, were among those who helped the crew of the Spanish supply ship *Il Gran Griffon*, part of the Armada, which was wrecked on Fair Isle, to return to Spain and received a silver cup in gratitude from the Duke of Medina Sidonia. The Balfours, after whom Balfour Place by the harbour is named, a different family, were not Fife lairds but local merchants. My family's grave is on the east path. On the west path is a sad, neglected well (at least I suppose it was a well) and by the walk lower down, the Blackwell grave. Finally by the gate out into the Punds is the grave of a family whose name I have never heard before or since – 'Corsanes'.

Beside the cathedral stands St Regulus' tower with the remains of his church. St Regulus is said to have brought the bones of St Andrew to this site. Scholars are in dispute about the exact date and origins of the church but it seems, however, that the tower – strongly reminiscent of Tuscany in style – was built in the late eleventh century. Walter Scott in his *Journal* tells how in old age he visited 'St Rules' tower'; unable to face climbing up it (as he had apparently always done on previous visits) he sat rather disconsolately on the bottom step. I sympathize with him. I have been unable to find out anything else about his visits to St Andrews and, indeed, only heard of this one through the good offices of Andrew Lang and Lionel Daiches.

The city was never enclosed by walls. Wynds and gardens joined the three main streets. The space in front of the cathedral where pilgrims and clerics must have gathered is still, except in the height of the tourist season, peaceful. Market Street does not reach the cathedral as it is closed by Castle Street and the house known as Dean's Court, a suitable building to grace the approaches to a cathedral. Castle Street has been well restored, making this medley of small houses at the end of Market Street one of the best bits of the town.

Up the Town – I

We start again in Abbotsford Crescent. It forms the concave side of a 'triangle' otherwise enclosed by a convex and a straight row of houses. The garden in the middle was always known as the square garden. 'The square', along presumably with Lockhart Place and Abbotsford Place, was completed about 1880 as a speculation by a parliamentary barrister called Hope. The streets were designed – quite well I think – by Chesser, an Edinburgh architect. Hope was first married to Miss Lockhart, Walter Scott's granddaughter – hence the Abbotsfords and Lockharts in the names. He later married a daughter of the Duke of Norfolk. He was a philanthropist, Liberal and friend of Gladstone – who may have invested money in the development.

The decent, if undistinguished, design of the square has been damaged by the insertion of dormer windows in the roofs – an understandable but ugly alteration we have seen already on many St Andrews houses. Less excusable is the removal of the mounting blocks which straddled the gutter of Abbotsford Crescent – the sort of pointless vandalism typical of some local authorities. It may be interesting to record the changes which have overtaken the square during my lifetime. Except for one house at the end of Hope Street and the large house at the east end of Abbotsford Crescent, every house was lived in by only one family. There was not a single guest-house nor, until after my uncle died at No. 10, Hope Street, a single rooming-house exclusively for students. Now, as throughout St Andrews, guest-houses and the university have taken over. The whole of Abbotsford Crescent is now a students' hostel.

At the west end of the Crescent lived Mr Pye, who dressed in breeches, kept white fan-tailed pigeons and a pack of beagles; whether he hunted them I do not know. Between Mr Pye and our house in the middle of the Crescent there dwelt the Barns-Grahams, the Wildes and the Currans. The Wildes were, I think, the last private family to live in the Crescent. Dodo Wilde and her mother refused to budge for all the frowns and the blandishments of Professor McIntosh and the university. The name Barns-Graham is now known because Miss Barns-Graham, a friend of my youth, has become a successful artist. They were really a county family, owning a property some 2 miles out of St Andrews. Two miles from St Andrews was in those days the equal of travelling fifty today. Miss Barns-Graham has never lived nor painted for long at St Andrews but the city can take some credit for her.

Further along the Crescent, next to us, lived the Currans, a family of which we saw a great deal and to whom we became related by marriage. Mr Curran was a precise, neat man with a piece missing out of his ear, who played golf in washed-leather gloves, sang, played the piano and translated Shakespeare into French. Nowadays he would no doubt demand a grant to enable him to pursue his hobby. Such a thought certainly never occurred to him then. Mrs Curran was a large, pale lady with a voice like a macaw but of genial disposition and I believe something of a wit. The only saying of hers that I remember being told was that on seeing me and her son, Geoffrey, who was older and bigger than I, coming up the aisle as pages at my sister's wedding, she remarked, 'Look, the camel yoked to the ass.' Of the Curran children, Desmond became a well-known psychiatrist, Lilian married Charles MacAndrew, the Deputy

Speaker of the House of Commons, later Lord MacAndrew, and Harry, after a chequered career, ended up as adviser to a Commonwealth government. Geoffrey, my friend, died rather young. Two of the most memorable features of the Curran household were, first, their nurse, 'Nannie Curran', an extraordinarily nice woman who presided over the most popular nursery in St Andrews, and, second, the hut in their garden furnished with cushions and an iron lantern which we thought romantic. An incident which gave Mrs Curran much pleasure was the remark made by a son of the Mappins of Mappin & Webb, aged about five, who came to tea one day, only to be turned from the door by Mrs Curran as Geoffrey had just developed measles. As he left, turning to his French nurse he remarked, 'C'est un peu trop fort.'

Our house, typical of the Crescent houses, was five storeys high including the basement. The basement contained the kitchen and scullery, the maids' sitting-room, the cook's bedroom, cellars and the back way out, much used as it led down to the links. In this 'room', which served as a passage to the back door, a bath had been installed. There was a separate lavatory outside and a wash-house or laundry. On the ground floor were the smoking-room, so-called even though my father had given up smoking and my mother only smoked in later life, the dining-room, pantry and a cloakroom and lavatory. On the first floor were my mother's bedroom and my father's dressing-room in which he had a small bath and hand basin but no lavatory. The drawing-room was on this floor looking north. There was also my bedroom. On the next floor were the day and night nurseries, two bedrooms and the only bathroom in which there was not only a bath, hand basin and lavatory but also a coal bunker. The only heating in the house was by coal fires (later supplemented by electric heaters). Most of the coal was flung through a hole in the pavement into a cellar in the 'area'. The coal men, however, also clumped up two flights of stairs and tipped a few sacks with a crash into the bathroom bunker; it was essential to keep the nursery fire going. A reproduction of a picture by Peter Graham of Highland cattle in a mist hung in the larger bedroom. It seems odd now that, though he was an RA, I do not think my family knew that he lived in St Andrews. Under the roof there were four more rooms but no water and, as far as I remember, no heating. Such was typical middle-class accommodation.

The back of the Crescent rises high and exposed to face the North. But I do not remember being very cold. My father and mother changed for dinner every night. There were never less than four servants; life was regular and comfortable. No cocktail parties. No gin. Neither my father nor mother drank except at dinner parties. If people came to dinner they were asked at a quarter to eight and arrived (in dinner jackets and long dresses) on the dot, to be offered sherry – and sherry only. I suppose some varieties of wine were drunk, but when my father died only a little champagne and vintage port were found in the cellar. Except for my married sister and her husband, few guests came to stay. St Andrews largely provided its own society. In turn, my parents seldom went away for short visits – and never for the weekend. Later when I was a boy and learnt to fish we sometimes went for a visit to Devon or Aberdeenshire. We had no car. A bus called for the heavy leather trunks and off we went from the station. After my father retired, long summer and Christmas visits to my sister and a month or two in the South of France broke into the year.

Next to us lived the Inglis family, whose son is a power in the world of Edinburgh trusts, and next to them the MacEwans and the Millers. Among the other residents in the square were my Uncle Foster, and an elderly Playfair colonel who shattered his eye-glass one day with my pop-gun! They lived at Nos 2 and

10 Hope Street, respectively. Professor McIntosh, our landlord, lived at No. 1. He bought most of the Crescent and presented it to the university – hence its present name of McIntosh Hall.

Between them at No. 8 lived St Andrews' leading seaman, Admiral Wilmot Nicolson. He was known as the 'wicked Wilmot': more a tribute to the general reputation of sailors than to any devilish trait in his character. Then came, at least for a time, the Skenes. Colonel Skene was a renowned St Andrews golfer, Captain of the Royal and Ancient in 1929. In that year Joyce Weltered, best of all women golfers, won the Captain's Prize on the Ladies' Putting Course. Helen Skene was a St Andrews beauty who married Murray Prain of another well-known Fife family and who has returned to the scenes of her youth. Some of these scenes were the games of rounders played on summer evenings in 'the square' garden. All games were meant to be forbidden in the garden, but the keepers of the garden had made the mistake of listing the forbidden games, and they had left out rounders. They had fallen into a trap well known to parliamentary draughtsmen. If you name everything that is banned then it is assumed that anything not named is allowed. Helen's brother, Dugald and I invented a game of 'trains' played on bicycles around the town, which was just the right size for it. His son is now an active Liberal Democrat politician.

The families of the square had without exception departed until my nephew bought a house in Hope Street very recently. One or two families have moved to other St Andrews houses, most to other climes. Some of them were my contemporaries and friends, such as the Hopwoods at No. 8 Howard Place. John Hopwood had a distinguished career in the army and his sister was a girlfriend of mine, who married Commander Wilson, one of the last directors of *Blackwood's Magazine*. The red-headed Waterston family also lived in Howard Place for a time. The father, Professor Waterston, had the distinction of being the sole British anatomist who detected from its discovery that 'Piltdown man' was a fake. His sons were doctors and good golfers, one son, David, became a foremost child doctor. Around the square Dr Miller could be seen riding a green bicycle with a hammock-like saddle and Dr Moir on his tricycle. The latter joined the St Andrews ghosts with remarkable expedition. As he lay on his deathbed he was 'seen' riding his tricycle in South Street – where he had previously lived in what is now the post office.

At the entrance to the square is the Hope Park Church, an impressive Gothic revival building built in 1864 by Peddie and Kinnear. Across the road from it stands another Scottish baronial Gothic building which used to be the Alexandra Hotel and was built by the architect, Jesse Hall. My younger sister claimed that she was born in it when my mother was on her way to the station. The closing of the station was a sad blow to old St Andrews' life. Outside it stood a row of cabs and buses. Until the Second World War the train was the main means of approach to the city and within it the main passenger transport was by bicycle or horse. Cars could be hired for longer journeys but I do not remember any 'taxi'. The station was a consider-able centre. The name 'St Andrews' was beautifully displayed by an arrangement of flowers and shells on the bank of the cutting in which the station lay. A hoist raised the luggage to street level; small boys could travel in it.

The railway officials were well known and respected local figures: the station master, Lees; the guard, Haddow; and Docherty, the foreman porter. Haddow was typical of the St Andrews functionaries. Immaculate in uniform and peaked cap he resembled a rather stout Sir Walter Scott. Docherty was more of Stevenson's build and colouring, and wore his cap on the back of his head. Both were men of standing and authority. I am glad that the spirit of the old railway men, helpful and humorous, still persists. Travelling recently in Fife in one of those trains laughably called Sprinters, I asked the ticket collector if it stopped at the Haymarket station in Edinburgh. 'Oh yes', he replied, 'it stops at every lamp-post.' When a boy I was reprimanded by Haddow for crossing the line to collect a starling's egg from a nest in the wall of the cutting. That evening after dark, Haddow called at our house and taking off his cap produced four eggs out of its crown. Quite a few people commuted to and from Dundee, either to University College, Dundee, then a part of St Andrews University, or to work in Dundee offices and mills. City Park, the house which looks down on the railway from the east, is another of Rae's designs.

Just beyond the station at the top of the city hill is a building, now much altered, but which seemed to carry an air of having been a chapel. Whether it once was I do not know, but it was the lair of Scott the joiner, a patriarchal figure whose dignified appearance was appropriate to the atmosphere of his workshop and his job of undertaker. He and his assistants wore long white smocks and pushed a hand-barrow. He was famous for his delays in coming to start a job and for the eternity of waiting for any repair job he removed to his sanctum. The smell of wood and glue and the deftness of his work with plane, saw or chisel fascinated children. I was also spell-bound listening to him and his assistants discussing the difficulty they would have in 'boxing' a well-known citizen when he died. The poor man was twisted with rheumatism and must indeed have presented what would now be called 'a challenge' to any undertaker.

Back-tracking past the Hope Park Church along St Mary's Place and Lockhart Place there used to be yet another church on the south side of the street. On the north side a respectable, if somewhat dreary, nineteenth-century house by Bryce in its own grounds has been demolished to make way for a new Students' Union built in the modern lumpish style, much uglier and even more dreary than old West Park. So we come to the crossroads where Greyfriars Gardens and Bell Street meet Market Street. On the south-west corner of the crossroads is the café once called the Victoria Café. It made the best ice-cream I have ever tasted. In the days before refrigeration its ice-cream used to be sent round to dinner parties. My family lived in this house before it became a café. Opposite, on the south-east corner, stood Mackies the drapers, who gave their name to the crossroads, known as Mackies Corner. I wonder what has happened to the bentwood chairs which stood along the counter so that shoppers could rest their legs and consider which ribbons or gloves or hats they should buy?

Had you passed this corner, the hinge of St Andrews (equivalent in its humble way to the crossroads of the Four Fountains in Palermo), on a winter's evening in the early 1920s, it is my contention that you might have heard youthful voices, fresh no doubt but untuneful, grating rather than floating from the windows above Mackies' shop. I remember the Skenes' French governess attempting to teach us 'Sur le pont d'Avignon' and 'Frère Jacques'. I also remember that it was in the flat above the shop. It just shows how legends begin. Helen Skene (Prain) tells me that her family certainly had a French governess, and she may well have done her best to carry French culture among the Philistine friends of the Skenes. Never, however, did the family live above Mackies. However, as I believe that how we see the world is a strong element in how it is, and myths are important to mankind, I shall continue to look up above Mackies' window and think of a group of recalcitrant small children under the benevolent but critical eye of 'Maddie'.

On the north-east corner was Kermath's the chemist, and a little way down Greyfriars Gardens came Sturrock's the hair-dressers and Methven Simpson's music shop where you could spend hours playing gramophone records. Lower down is one of the few surviving shops of old St Andrews – Piries, who sell crockery and have retained their shop front. Nearer still to North Street is a seller of maps and good second-hand books – a necessary amenity in a university town.

Mackies Corner marked the beginning of the shopping centre for those who lived further west. If you said that you were going 'up the town', that meant to the east of Mackies. Bell Street leading to South Street contained a fine range of shops. On the east side you passed Howies, the toy shop, and Mrs Foster, an antiques dealer in whose back shop I once found lurking my friend, Frank Prince, the poet. He was a relation of hers. Then came Reid, the jewellers. Further up towards South Street was Jesse Hall's Congregational Church, now demolished; the adjoining buildings have been so adroitly sewn together, so to speak, that it might never have existed. Then came a draper, Donaldson, before you reached another Donaldsons, this time the bootmakers. On the opposite corner of the opening into South Street was Aikman Terras, leading grocers, whose shop interior has been resurrected by the Preservation Society in the house we have already visited at the east end of North Street. The closure of the shop must, however, be a great loss to St Andrews; like Robertson's and Haxton & Grubb's it was a proper grocer with polished counters and glass biscuit boxes, bins and chests of drawers labelled for spices, teas, etc. The assistants wore long aprons and the shop was filled with the smell of roasting coffee. As someone, Ngaio Marsh I think, has pointed out, the best coffee in the world never tastes quite as good as its smell. Coming down Bell Street on the west side there was a newspaper shop kept by two Miss Flouds, a small family newsagent of a type now almost extinct. One of the Miss Flouds, for I presume it was she, sat knitting behind the counter on which slept her cat; she was a friend of my nurse who regularly called to collect *The*

Quiver while I, no doubt, picked up *The Rainbow* or *Tiger Tim's Weekly*. Next to it, after the war, was the chemist, Leith's. Mr Leith has had a remarkable career, having been a colonel in the army, a chemist and a minister of the Church of Scotland, presiding at one time over the parish of Firth in Orkney.

Going back to Mackies Corner we continue our walk up Market Street. On the north side there were two dairies of a type which, like old-fashioned grocers, have almost vanished: the Maypole and the Buttercup; spotless, tiled shops with china cows in the window. On the left before the Buttercup was M.P. Reid, a draper, a small draper with an even smaller message-boy. All St Andrews shops in the 1920s delivered messages, most by bicycle, some on foot. The message-boys whistled and rang their bells, adding to the gaiety of the streets.

I have never been wholly opposed to the employment of children. In some factories it was often no doubt appalling. But what was the alternative? – either sitting in some small, dark room or being at school. Children don't, on the whole, much like school and in any case schooling in the nineteenth century was often brief and cruel, so a round of visits on foot or bicycle must have been quite welcome. We were brought up on the legend that American senators and presidents began their working lives by delivering newspapers. Things do not seem to have improved much since they dropped this start to life.

The tiny message-boy of M.P. Reid often reached our house in the dark after tea. He could hardly reach the letter-box even if his package for delivery would go into it. So the bell would be rung – apparently no one there – then a little voice about the level of one's knees announced 'M.P. Reid' and the parcel would be handed over. It was occasionally suggested that our letter-box should be lowered. For some years we had a table maid who could not reach into the wire basket, so she would hurry out with a chair. Sometimes out of gallantry my father would carry the chair. The table maid would then climb onto it, collect the letters, place them on a wooden salver and hand them to him. But the letter-box was never lowered.

Next on this side was Johnston's garage and stables, one of the two principal stables in the city. Apart from the cabs and buses, horses were in demand for riding. Johnston's horses lived on the first floor up a wooden stair, making a fine clatter going up and down. Rutherford, Son and Grubb, Coal Merchants, displayed in their window two or three neatly carved miniature wagons filled with coal. Passing the Cross Keys Hotel, an ancient tavern now defunct, you come to two banks, the Royal Bank of Scotland and a branch of the Bank of Scotland which used to be the British Linen Bank or 'Bank of the British Linen Company', as its branch in Cupar was inscribed, a reminder of how important the flax trade and linen industries were to Fife. Until the 1950s there were eight Scottish joint stock banks, of which three survive.

The manager of a shoe shop on the other side of the street recently bought a shoe shop in Blairgowrie. Among the stock he found an elegant but old-fashioned pair of shoes, size 1. He told me that they had been made-to-measure for a cousin of mine who, on being told that they would cost 27s. 6d., exclaimed that she could not wear such expensive shoes so never collected them, nor had his successor ever found a customer who could wear shoes of that size. On the corner of College Street John Macgregor carried on business as 'Cabinet Maker, Upholsterer, Undertaker, Auctioneer, Valuator and House Factor'. The medieval town house, regrettably demolished by order of Provost Playfair, stood here. To be fair to the provost, it must be said that he preferred to save it, but Aikman, the grocer, was adamant that it must go.

The fountain in the middle of Market Street is a memorial to Whyte Melville, writer and foxhunter, who lived at Mount

Melville and was for many years Master of the Fife foxhounds and a prominent golfer. Andrew Lang wrote that it was, 'Much like two large breakfast cups suspended over a still larger slop basin on which a round white medallion bears a profile in relief . . . The profile will recall Lord Dundreary.' A market of plants, flowers and vegetables used to be held around the fountain. The water has now been turned off and the cups and slop basin filled with earth. Why, I do not know; unless it is the town's final blow at the students who used to splash in its waters, fuelling the hate side of the love-hate relationship which from the earliest times bound the town to its university.

This may be a suitable moment to consider the famous (or notorious) mid-nineteenth-century provost, Sir Hugh Lyon Playfair. Widely known as 'the Major' in honour of his army career, he came to St Andrews from India and brought many acquired habits with him. He is accused of treating St Andrews like one of the Indian towns which he controlled. He did much for golf and it is said he was a very fair performer (unlike many Playfairs). We can all applaud his sanitary reforms. If he left the town less picturesque it was at least cleaner and it is only those who do not live in them who admire slum houses. In many ways, however, he went too far, his nephew Lord Playfair recording how, 'Ancient stairs which projected from the houses into the streets so as to block the thoroughfares were removed during the darkness of night and the occupants had to devise new modes of entrance.' He seems to have been an enthusiast for street lighting and broad sidewalks. For an account of him, you should read *Hugh Lyon Playfair (1786–1868): A Reappraisal*, by Alan L. Pride. We shall visit the site of his eccentric garden later.

On the south side of the street at the corner of Logies Lane, which leads to South Street and the Town Kirk, stood Wilson's, the greengrocer's shop, the selling arm for the market garden in Greenside Place. The founder of this business was John Wilson who started as gardener to Provost Playfair in Abbey Walk. A little further along, abutting on the widening of the street into the market-place, hung the swinging sign of a large golden boot, trademark of Hogg's Fife Boots. Round the corner from Hogg's stood Grubb, the grocer (another 'Happy Families' reminder), which had a round window, sacks and sawdust on the floor. The tenement next to it must surely be seventeenth or eighteenth century in origin, though no doubt much restored.

Church Street joins Market Street to South Street and like its twin, Bell Street, was, and still is, full of good shops. On the western corner in a building by Gillespie-Scott was one of Henderson's two shops. W.C. Henderson were the chief booksellers in St Andrews; their main bookshop was further up Church Street on the left. Other noteworthy shops on either side of the street were Niven the butchers – two Nivens who were said not to be on speaking terms. Martins, also butchers (who according to their 1902 advertisement not only delivered but called for orders) and Gordon, the fishmonger, where Miss Evans was a queen among shopkeepers, large, jolly, a martinet and a very good fishmonger. There appears to have been a plethora of butchers in St Andrews before the First World War – three or four in Church Street alone. On the right-hand side of the street stood the St Andrews Savings Bank, a local institution in which I had my first bank account, now amalgamated with other savings banks. The public library looks out on the square, overpowered by the town church.

Among the shops on the left or east side of the street you could find, down an alley, a tinsmith; I suppose today he would be turned out as the area is not 'zoned' for industry. Along with carpenters, such as Scott and Thom the club-makers, the blacksmith's forge and a mason, he was one of the few small businesses in the town. Such artisans make cities lively. Their expulsion to industrial estates is a great mistake. Workmen were marked not only by the tools of their trade but by their appearance, bakers were covered with flour and the coalmen and Haggerty the chimney sweep had their faces lined with black like badly made-up minstrels.

Beyond the mouth of Church Street you until recently came to another of the very few shops surviving with the same name and premises from between the wars. The Fairfield Stores, alas, even as this book goes to print, has died. Also in this street was a celebrated butchers – an admirable butcher whose meat was always properly hung. Unfortunately, it appears some arsenic found its way into his sausages one day with serious consequences for his customers. There was at least one death and my uncle was confined to bed for several days. Such, however, was the butcher's good reputation and that of his produce that his trade hardly suffered. The shop closed long ago.

The east end of Market Street narrows into a street flanked by some charming small houses, one of which, a plain eighteenth- or early nineteenth-century plastered house, is one of my favourite St Andrews houses. Opposite is a new court named after Miss Kidston, who was a leader of intellectual life and a battler for the preservation of old buildings in St Andrews. She was one of those energetic, public-spirited, middle-aged ladies upon whom British civilization so much depends. Without much money or any official position she undertook all sorts of good works. Among other things she did something to preserve the memory of the Mackenzie sisters, whose woodcuts are one of the few works of art produced in modern St Andrews.

Castle Street, which we met at the end of the Scores and also at All Saints' Church, is one of the best preserved of the old streets. Several buildings still retain outside stairs, a peculiarly

Scottish feature, and its houses reflect the warmth and variation of sandstone. In the old days when a few fishermen still survived it was tumbledown: now it has risen in the world with fresh paint and ornaments in the windows.

If you visit St Andrews in August you may find the main streets – South Street and Market Street, Bell Street and Church Street – blocked by the Lammas Fair. This fair, like the Senzie Mart Fair, goes back to the Middle Ages. It would have been primarily an autumn market. Unlike the other fair it was largely a local event. It was also no doubt a feeing market when farmers came to hire farm servants for the coming year. Now it is an amusement fair and dozens of booths and roundabouts clog the streets. In the past, parties would be arranged to visit the fair in the evenings. Children would be supplied with extra pocket money, some of which would go to buy or win the china ornaments of which we were justly proud. I do not remember dancing in the streets. To judge by the clothes in the photograph, it seems to have reached its zenith rather earlier than my time. Grown-ups performed prodigies of strength by hitting a contraption with a sledge-hammer which drove a weight up a scale like a barometer. Benny Lynch the boxer was photographed at it. If it rained as, of course, it must frequently have done, the fair was spoilt. Yet I do not remember many disappointments, nor do I remember the residents of South and Market streets complaining of the noise and disruption. The booths tailed away towards the east end of South Street, no doubt in deference to the numerous professors and colonels who lived there.

Up the Town – II

The West Port is an obvious place from which to start a walk up South Street. But before passing through it or its postern gate we should glance at the Drill Hall to the North, built of local brick to the design of Hall. It was a centre for badminton which was a great St Andrews game. There under the wide and lofty roof three courts were filled two or three times a week with children and women; few men seemed to play as far into middle age as their spouses, who were spotlessly turned out in white. There too, 'A' squadron of the 2nd Fife & Forfar Yeomanry were stationed at the start of the Second World War under the command of Major Brown of the Argyle mineral water factory. The 2nd Fife & Forfar owed a lot to Major Brown, a veteran of the first war, as upright as a guardsman and a very nice man. This fine body of men marched off early in the war to Cupar and were seen no more in the nursery of their squadron. I went to Cupar by bus, forbidden to march as I had no uniform.

On the south-west corner of the crossroads stands the Whey Pat Tavern – rather a good building bearing a name I never heard elsewhere. Down the road a little, on the left as you go south, the blacksmith's forge used to blaze. Now nothing more exciting than a garage stands near its romantic cavern. Cart-horses and bellows have ebbed to a legacy of motorcars and petrol pumps.

The West Port itself has somehow escaped destruction.

Andrew Lang confidently foretold that the City Fathers would knock it down to make way for trams, but the trams have never come. However, even without them the Town Council demolished the gate in North Street. Being neither particularly beautiful nor of any religious significance, it has escaped the improvers and the reformers. It is not impressive as a fortification, being much restored, chiefly in the nineteenth century, and giving more the impression of stage scenery than a medieval gateway. However, it makes a good introduction to South Street, the main street of St Andrews, a wide and impressive thoroughfare ending about half a mile away at the cathedral. At this gate Charles II received the keys of the city and it is, I believe, the only gate to survive in any Scottish city.

Immediately on the right as you pass through stands a handsome building by Milne, under which was the Blue Bell Tavern. This was a favourite place of refreshment for 'A' squadron during our short stay in the Drill Hall and featured in our song 'I saw him, I saw him, lying on the Blue Bell floor I saw him.' In bygone days St Andrews seems to have been well supplied with taverns: there were forty-two in 1793 for a population of some 2,500.

Leading south off South Street are two or three wynds which still retain their old cottages, one of which in Loudens Close is the first piece of restoration carried out by the St Andrews Preservation Trust. On the north side, too, most of the oldish houses remain, including MacArthurs the bakers. Sixty years ago MacArthurs had two shops in South Street, the other being at the east end of the street on the corner of Abbey Street. They made delicious meringue-like cakes called (I do not know why) Japanese cakes. Just before Bell Street, next door to what was Aikman Terras, Wilson the ironmonger still looks out through ordinary house windows. The interior has changed. It used to have flagstone floors and smelt of oil and twine.

35 A St Andrews butcher's display

36 Nineteenth-century shop fronts in South Street, with houses from an earlier date behind

37   The shop of Mr Wilson in South Street where golf clubs and other golfing equipment could be purchased before the Second World War

38   Kinburn House

39   The house in Burgher's Close where the Burgher congregation met

40 The east end of South Street with my nephew, Mark Black, in the foreground

41 Looking through the gateway at the top of the Pends

42 Two of the smaller Boothby owls from Balmacarron, now perched in South Street

43   Upper Ladebraes burn, with ducks

44   Old cottages by the Ladebraes burn near Kilrymont

45 A typical plain and satisfactory St Andrews house of the late nineteenth century at the top of Abbey Walk

46 Dempster Terrace

On the other side of the road stand the Baptist church and a building which was once Suttie's lemonade works. Next to them is the ruin of the Blackfriars monastery, another monument to Knox and his rapacious gang. But behind it the Madras College is the best post-Reformation building in the city. Built by Burn it can hardly be faulted. Well proportioned, it is an excellent example of semi-Tudor, semi-classical architecture, a distinctive Scots style which flourished in the earlier part of the last century. It is more lively than the St Salvator's buildings of Nixon and Reid which were its contemporaries. The founder of the college, the Revd Dr Bell, was a benefactor to Scottish education in the class of Andrew Carnegie and in addition an educational reformer. He was born in St Andrews but ended his career as a Prebendary of Westminster. He devised a system of education which depended upon the older children teaching the younger. Thus a shortage of teachers could be remedied by 'monitors' trained to assist in the elementary classes. He not only endowed the Madras College but gave a considerable sum to spread the system he favoured in Edinburgh, Glasgow, Aberdeen, Leith and Inverness and the Royal Naval School.

Dr Bell's supporters were caught up in a tiresome row with those of Joseph Lancaster over who invented the Madras or monitorial system. Bell stood for the Episcopalians – Scots and English – Lancaster for the Free Churchmen. Both were ultimately pushed into hot water for trying to get education on the cheap – usually by those for whom any reduction in price is anathema. Perhaps in their day any education was better than the alternative which was too often none. As for teaching by the older boys, it depends on the subject and the boys. Beckford when aged five certainly gained from being taught music by Mozart, who was nine at the time. Dr Bell came by his money rather dubiously (chiefly by speculation in tobacco and the accumulation of sinecures) but disposed of it well and St Andrews is rightly grateful to him.

Those who would like to know more about the Madras system and a row famous in its day should read the *History of Elementary School Contest in England* by Francis Adams. It is entertainingly written and contains several sprightly quotations. Opinions grew heated on both sides. Coleridge found 'Celestial marvels both in the scheme and the men' (Bell). Of one of the more violent contenders on the Bell side, Sydney Smith wrote, 'A lady of respectable opinions and very moderate talents defending what is right without judgement and believing what is holy without charity.'

Nowadays the altruism and optimism of both Lancaster and Bell seem breathtaking. We live in an age cluttered with technology when nevertheless we cannot find money to pay our own teachers properly, still less to educate mankind. In a much poorer age, Lancaster was confident that with his system he could educate the world – and with vast optimism but little sense he raised large sums of money for this purpose, even from the royal family. Dr Bell merely set out to educate Britain and convert India to Christianity. Both believed that universal Christian education (but only non-conformist Christian on one side, and Episcopalian Christian on the other) would transform the world. In Dr Bell's favour it has to be said that non-conformists (along with some non-Christians) were admitted to his schools. We have indeed lost the optimism, the belief in individual responsibility and individual perfectability, the belief in the power of education and the unselfishness of both Bell and Lancaster. As Francis Adams wrote:

A few million more or less spent on a foreign war, or in reducing a rebellious colony or in chastising some wretched hordes of savages [or, he might have written since the demise of empire, of raising the salaries of top people, increasing the bureaucracy or government advertising] are never taken gravely into account in our method of government but every penny required for raising the condition of the people has always been voted with reluctance.

Dr Bell reckoned that 7s. 6d. per year would educate a child. Those who, like myself, pin our hopes on education must be open to disillusion when we see the incompetence which seems to be spreading from top to bottom in spite of universal schooling.

Walking along the south side of South Street you come next to a rather distinguished building by Rae in his sober eighteenth-century style far removed from the turreted fancies of Edgecliffe. This house, before it became a university staff club, was the Royal Hotel. It was one of the better hotels. In Hay Fleming's guide of 1902 it offered lunches starting at 1 p.m. for 2s. At the back of it were McNally's stables which were, along with Johnston's in Market Street, the chief abode of horses in St Andrews. Most of McNally's were riding horses. And so on past another 'bespoke' tailor, who sat cross-legged on his counter, to Queens Gardens.

On the north side of the street going east from Bell Street, a line of shops included Coopers and Mr King, a wine merchant, whose window screen bore the names of Hill, Thomson, Wauchope Moodie, and Cockburn & Campbell – Edinburgh wine merchants for whom he was agent. For some reason they greatly intrigued me. Mr King, a small, busy man in a Homburg hat, hardly looked the swashbuckling smuggler which I imagined all wine merchants to be.

You should glance down Burgher Lane because it has a well-restored house at the end and was the site of the Burgher Church. The Burghers played a leading part in one of the innumerable schisms of the Presbyterian Church. They were the forerunners of the congregation of Hope Park Church – the start of our next walk.

On this side of South Street you will find some old small houses which survive behind nineteenth-century shop fronts with cast-iron pillars. Then you come to the general post office, once the home of the Moirs before they moved to Howard Place. Before he became a ghost Dr Moir had founded the Cottage Hospital. The family provided the first woman provost of the town and, in its day a great distinction, were related to Douglas Jardine the cricketer. The general post office, like the railway station, was a centre of St Andrews life. Next came Mrs Taylor, a rival 'modiste' to Miss Pringle and Lucille Morny of Greyfriar's Gardens. Mrs Taylor offered to get you (if you were a woman) a suit 'cut in London'. Then comes the rather agreeable, almost art nouveau, front of what used to be Fletchers. Fletchers is another building by those ubiquitous architects of all styles – Gillespie and Scott. It nowadays would be called a gift shop I suppose: it sold high-class stationery, ornaments, blotters and a few books of what are now the coffee-table variety. In its advertisement for 1902 it also included gongs, a testimony to the age of domestic servants. What is now Boots was even then the town's largest chemist, Smith & Govan, replete with large jars of coloured glass and smaller jars of blue and white china.

We have now reached the centre of the town, a small square lying to the north of South Street almost entirely filled by the Town Kirk. This medieval building was repaired, indeed largely rebuilt, in the eighteenth century and was again restored by Macgregor Chalmers at the instigation of Dr Patrick Playfair. Like the activities of his relative, the provost, the work has been criticized as too drastic. In particular it is said that the vaulted stone roof need not have been demolished. But today after it has mellowed it seems pretty good if, like all Presbyterian churches, a trifle scrubbed, though not as bad as most. Chalmers copied features from several medieval churches, as explained in Dr Cant's pamphlet 'The Restoration of Holy Trinity Church, St Andrews 1907–1909'. As with so many churches, the activities of modern thieves have meant that it has to be kept locked but if you can get in, it holds the seventeenth-century monument to Archbishop Sharp, murdered at Magus Muir on the way to Ceres. It is a fine black and white piece of carving made in Holland.

Across South Street on the east corner of Queens Gardens stands the Scottish baronial-style town hall designed by Hamilton, an Edinburgh architect, and built in 1858–61. It has one of those turreted bay windows cantilevered out on the corner in a manner beloved by the Scots. Meant to be impressive, it succeeds and has an equally successful hall inside it where functions such as the Golf Ball, a highlight of the autumn season of the Royal and Ancient, took place. You will see a plaque let in to the wall of the town hall, commemorating the stay of the Polish forces in St Andrews during the Second World War. They caused a considerable flutter. The local women and girls enjoyed their company, but the local men were not so sure. But they behaved extremely well. From here up to the cathedral, South Street has retained great character, making it one of the more pleasant streets in Scotland.

The history of St Andrews since the Reformation is sad. Its great buildings destroyed and its heroes and heroines, such as Mary Queen of Scots and Montrose, executed or murdered. Boswell and Johnson found it dispiriting to see this ancient Archiepiscopal city sadly deserted, and Andrew Lang writes of it with love certainly but also with grief. Its university spent long, poverty-stricken years after the fall of the old religion with a handful of students living among an even more poverty-stricken population. Scotland might have possessed one richer and bigger university if it had moved to Perth – as it nearly did.

I believe that in spite of the horrible crimes she suffered and the spoliation of her beauties, the plight of St Andrews from the point of view of the ordinary citizen may have been exaggerated. The idea of open sewers and middens in the streets is unattractive. These were common, however, in many towns of the seventeenth and eighteenth centuries. Open sewers in which the refuse ran may have been rather more sanitary than stagnant underground pools. The air, though piercing, is said to have been healthy. St Andrews was comparatively free from plague. Mr Smart has unearthed a tribute to St Andrews from a Professor Pringle refusing blandishments to get him to move to Edinburgh:

Here I am lodged to my mind I eat to my mind in a regular collegiate manner. Here I am always at hand when business calls supported in the exercise of it by the happy Remains of Ancient wholesome discipline of which there is scarcely a vestige with you nor can there be where Scholars live in town separated from the watchful eye of the master. Here I live in a healthful place sweet and clean surrounded by gardens (and these peopled with the cheerful thrush and other small choristers of the air). Quiet ample fields for exercise and diversions.

Boswell and Johnson enjoyed their visit and remarked upon a non-juring clergyman (supposedly outlawed) 'strutting about in his canonicals with a jolly countenance.' Boswell noted with malicious pleasure that the keys of the university library could not be found. They did, however, visit St Leonard's College by candlelight.

In my youth I believe St Andrews was a happy town, not

only for me and my well-off contemporaries, but even for poorer children. Nor were they over-awed by the rich. Walking up Castle Street early this century in a new suit as a boy, Sir Edward Playfair was greeted with cries of 'Gentry Pup' and pelted with mussel shells. There were, of course, sad people. At the end of Hope Street lived a lame man who took his slightly deranged son every day to the school where he was ragged and bullied. The social services have done something for such people. There were also many poor families. There were bare-footed children and women in shawls. But they played hop-scotch in the streets, had friendly neighbours and perhaps did not suffer the degradation of city slum dwellers to the same extent. As for the richer children, St Andrews was a delight. Miss Robertson, the grocer, gave me a bar of chocolate when I called with my mother and the blacksmith made no effort to drive us from the fascination of his roaring forge.

Here lies the heart of St Andrews. As you go east both sides of the street should be examined. On the left as we go towards the cathedral we pass the rather appealing bogus Tudor front of the *Citizen* office. The father of Bell of Madras College worked here as a printer; the site has connections with printing and publishing which date back many years. Like many local papers, the *St Andrews Citizen* is a fount of interest and a mine of information past and present. It should not be missed. The houses on the north side are good, solid buildings going back in parts for three or four centuries, but mostly presenting eighteenth- or nineteenth-century fronts to the street. From them two closes lead north to Market Street. They are worth peering down. On the east side of Crail Lane stood a rickety building with bulging pink plaster and a head in a night-cap 'appliquéd' to the wall. I believed, wrongly apparently, that it was the meeting place of the Knights Templar. The head has vanished to be replaced by a burglar or fire alarm. According to

Professor Read, a much more reliable authority than I, the Knights Templar or Hospitalers house was the building in South Street with pillars on either side of the door, now the home of the Department of Medieval History. Before it housed Medieval History it was the home of a remarkable historian or archaeologist, the Revd Professor Baxter of St Mary's College. Owing to his favourable standing that he had somehow acquired with the Turkish Government, he was able to excavate a site in Asia Minor, causing envy and chagrin to archaeologists who considered themselves better qualified.

Further along the street No. 41 has a good balcony and, I am glad to say, as after all this is a university town, you also pass an attractive second-hand bookseller. Janetta's the Italian ice-cream-seller stood beyond it. I am surprised that no one seems to have written a thesis on the Italian ice-cream families in Scottish towns. You could have found one or more families in every town from Shetland to the borders. How did they hear of such towns? How did they divide up their territories? Above all, how did they come to terms with the climate? On the corner of Castle Street stood Glass's Tavern where Boswell and Johnson lodged. Their visit was a success. The professors put up with Johnson's didactic dogmatism. If the visitors found the town sad, this was only by comparison with its past glory. They, like many others, reflected upon the tragic destruction of the cathedral. They were a cerebral pair, of course, without much power of observation. They complained of missing St Regulus' Tower, a rather large building in a prominent position, because no one brought it to their attention. Professor Rose, before moving to the Scores, lived at No. 7. Later, Colonel and Mrs MacAllan also lived at No. 7. He and his brother had married sisters – the Misses Wedderburns who added much to St Andrews life. They were jolly, forthcoming ladies endowed with formidable energy and a great deal of conversation, as one might expect as they were descended from Wedderburn, Earl of Rosslyn, an eighteenth-century Lord Chancellor.

Right at the end of South Street stands a block of more striking houses, one of which, the Roundel, is distinguished by a round tower. I like their russet stone, their quiet and their distinction. The Roundel, which was the first house of Dr Paton and his wife, has been the home of various professors, such as Professor Williams who was Professor of History: a tall, thin man whose wife played right-handed badminton wearing a leather glove on her left hand. Later, Professor Woozley of Moral Philosophy lived there. He was a great friend of mine from Oxford. A Fellow of All Souls', he ended up at the University of Virginia. In spite of family troubles he carried an air of perpetual youth. Like all the best academics I have known he was meticulous in the study of his subject but encouraged his mind to range outside it. In his heyday, university teachers did not seem so ground down by administration and the need to publish as they are today. We have now reached Dean's Court, which we saw from the end of North Street with another pleasant garden and trees behind it.

South Street itself gains greatly from its trees. They were planted at the suggestion of Milne the architect. Some complain that they are too drastically pruned, but anyone who has lived under the shade of big trees will sympathize. If you go for a walk in St Andrews you should take with you the Preservation Trust's pamphlet on its trees written by Professor MacDonald – *Trees in St Andrews*. It adds to the pleasure of wandering round the town. The professor lists over 260 species of tree, which puts paid to the libel that trees will not grow in Scotland. Many are fine single specimens but there are also pleasant clumps and rows as on the Ladebraes (also largely due to Milne), at Rathelpie and the botanic gardens.

Here we cross the road to inspect the great ruined gatehouse which leads to the Pends. Then we turn back past Queen Mary's House, taking care to pass through the postern in which you are entitled to a wish. The front of Queen Mary's facing South Street is distinguished if rather severe; the back has more variety and charm. The house now belongs to St Leonard's School. I will not attempt to describe it. Its point is that it is a beautiful if austere domestic building with the aura of a palace. You will not find such houses outside Scotland though, in an entirely different style of architecture, the townhouses of such continental cities as Aix give the same feeling. Enough has been written about Queen Mary and her St Andrews story. If you can trespass into the house, do so, it has delightful rooms and garden. When visiting the library and asking what the girls read, I was told 'accounts of first war battles, particularly bayonet charges.'

Going west we cross the road which leads to Crail and the coast. The east side of it has been pulled down for road widening, removing a row of cottages which masked the rather nondescript school building behind. On the corner with South Street stood MacArthurs, the baker's second shop. In Abbey Street stands the tiny Byre Theatre, so called because its buildings were part of one of St Andrews' farms. Elliot Playfair, who lived in Windmill Road and Abbotsford Place, used to direct and act near it. As he stammered his success on the stage was a tribute to the Playfair devotion to acting.

From MacArthur's shop to St Mary's College stands a row of late seventeenth- or eighteenth-century houses of almost complete domestic perfection. They are neither grand nor spectacularly beautiful, but infinitely pleasing. Everything about them – their variety within their unity, their stone, the design of their windows, their brass bell pulls – fits in together and welcomes the eye. I can imagine that they are the despair of architects. An architect on seeing them may well reflect, 'With all my training I shall never do better than these.' In them have lodged many notable men – pre-eminent in my memory is Professor D'Arcy Thompson, No. 44 South Street. He was a Professor of Natural History in St Andrews and Dundee for over sixty years. Apart from the subject of his professorship he was an authority on the birds of ancient Greece. With his brown beard and slouch hat he looked like a nineteenth-century portrait of a Royal Academician. He was the best-known St Andrews sight of my youth, every inch a professor of the old school. He had two beautiful and musical daughters who gave good nursery teas, after one tea party the professor presented me with two stuffed birds. Dr Cant has a story about Professor Thompson travelling in a tram in Dundee when a drunk man coming to sit beside him announced, 'You'r a verra learned man, Professor Thompson, but I ken something ye dinna ken.' D'Arcy affected not to hear but when the statement had been repeated several times he responded grumpily, 'Very well, what is it you know that I don't know?' 'My wife washes tae yer wife,' the man replied, 'and I hae on yin o' yer sarks [shirts].'

The Graces, the leading St Andrews lawyers, whom we will meet again later, had No. 60 as their townhouse. No. 58 was Captain Burn, the grandfather of the Macallams and, in spite of his comparatively low rank, a leader of the retired officers. A man who had some pretensions to dispute the captain's claim to be the 'father' of the Royal and Ancient withdrew on over-hearing Captain Burn casually remark to an acquaintance that the summer (sometime in the 1920s) was the best he could remember since 1850. At No. 56 lived the Professor of English, Professor Blyth Webster, and at No. 54 Professor Forrester, a theologian. No. 52 was inhabited by a mere medical doctor but a popular one (all the St Andrews doctors of my youth seemed to be popular) Dr McKerrow.

The backs of these houses – if 'backs' is the proper description for the sides which face south over the gardens – have been much altered. The gardens, however, may come as a revelation. They extended all the way down to Queen's Terrace, over 300 yards. Though several have been curtailed by having houses or garages built at their far end, they are still substantial and together form a world which might be in the country. In one of these is a fine yew, perhaps too fine for it blocks the light. In another is an avenue of pear trees. Beyond the pear trees in the garden at No. 46 stands an early eighteenth-century dovecote. It is a most sketchable building. The bottom floor of what was once the home of pigeons has been made into a sitting-room for humans and is frescoed. As these long gardens would up to the last century have given on open country the pigeons could forage far and wide.

So we come to St Mary's College, whose history you will find in the books of Dr Cant and Professor Read. Facing South Street is the Laigh Parliament Hall, so called because the Scots Parliament once met therein. On the floor of the Upper Hall a meridian of longitude is marked by a line, taken by observations from the window to a plinth set up on the hill above the site of what was Mount Melville railway station a mile to the south near the road to Crail. I am told by Dr Cant that the plinth still lies in a nearby farmyard.

With the university was associated the family of Gregory, distinguished mathematicians and astronomers in the seventeenth and eighteenth centuries. James Gregory, who corresponded with Newton, was the first Professor of Mathematics in the university. His elder brother fathered thirty-two children. Among other students of St Andrews University in the eighteenth century, when it reached its low point in numbers and wealth, was James Wilson, who was a native of the parish of Ceres. He became a leading lawyer in Pennsylvania, highly influential as a statesman and a signatory to the Declaration of Independence and the Constitution of the USA. Even in its dark days the university had its distinguished teachers and alumni.

Through the gate of the college you come into one of the most pleasant courts of any university, with a large holm oak in the middle and to your right a thorn said to have been planted by Queen Mary. The eighteenth-century residence of the principal, another of St Andrews' best buildings, is on your right. I should much like to have been principal of St Mary's in the days when the principal lived in that excellent house and the college had some two or three dozen students. But you had to be a minister of religion, for St Mary's is the theological college. It used to be said that there were five professors of theology and ten students; an exaggeration no doubt, but a fault on the right side. The decline of theology and philosophy at universities is deplorable. To your left, on the east side, was the university library before the new monster off North Street was built. Part of it was designed by Lorimer in a vaguely classical style but it has been hacked about and is now not very impressive. Penetrate a little further and you will find the relic of an old gateway and, more rewarding, on the south gable of the principal's house a pear tree. In September on the ground below it are scattered rather good, small pears which the university does not bother to collect – so why shouldn't you?

Argyle,
Rathelpie and
Beyond

We start for the west from the Hope Park Church which we have seen before. From it we go along the Double Dykes. The name is, I am told, a corruption of some derogatory description such as the 'Aberdumsey's Dumps'. Before the railway was abandoned you crossed a cutting just after leaving City Park house on your right. From the cutting you could look down on the station. You are now approaching the district of Rathelpie – a Pictish name.

Immediately to the west of the station stands Kinburn House in its grounds of several acres. Nothing could sound more Scottish than 'Kinburn', but I am told that its sound is misleading. It was built for a Dr Buddo who had been a surgeon in the army and he christened it after a fort in the Crimea. Dr Buddo came to a sad end. He shot dead a boy who he thought was stealing apples in his garden and himself died insane as a result. In my youth, Kinburn belonged to a Miss Patterson, a short, square and rather forbidding woman who wore a fur boa. Perhaps she inherited a certain trigger-happiness for she used to pay boys to shoot sparrows. Kinburn is the sort of property which seems doomed to become municipal; a rather gloomy, baronial house with a tower at each corner set in depressing evergreen shrubs. Now, however, it shelters putting greens and tennis courts. As the hard-court championship of Scotland, the Kinburn tournament in August was a considerable St Andrews event. My sisters were keen players and winners. The Collins brothers used to stay with us. They were notable athletes, especially Ian who, despite having broken a leg playing soccer for Oxford, was a scratch golfer. He was never beaten when in partnership with Colin Gregory in the Davies Cup and was once the victor over Cochet at Wimbledon. He was an attractive man with an upturned nose, rather gaunt face and expressive eyes. He was popular and intelligent with a flair for life and, of course, publishing. How he knew the value of books, though, was a mystery to me as he was seldom seen to read one; no doubt his native shrewdness helped. He was one of those men who had become indoc-trinated by the English public school system to promote physical rather than mental abilities. Many such men, including Ian, found congenial work in some of the more eccentric units and semi-private armies of the last war. His brother Billy was also a good tennis player and probably a better publisher.

On the opposite side of the Double Dykes, before you come to Kinburn, lived Bella Lindsay in a wooden hut. She had vaguely aristocratic connections and was presumably badly off. Neither circumstance seemed to depress or inhibit her. Dressed in a rig-out of black shawls, black satin dresses, jet bangles and a toque or bonnet, she talked continuously in a high cackle which went well with her brown, wizened face. Small and lively she was a popular, though somewhat alarming, figure at bridge parties. Her gossip was disrespectful, her comments caustic. In the street her greetings were fired off at a range of 20 yards accompanied by gestures which were rather startling to children. However, she frequently produced sweets out of the recesses of her muff or swathes of miscellaneous clothing. My parents were somewhat nervous of the sweets for Bella was none too clean and her hut smelt villainously of cat. Margot Asquith, when I later met her, reminded me of her. The railway cutting has now been filled in and a car park has to my great regret supplanted Bella Lindsay's hut. Further up on the same side stand Kinburn East and Kinburn West, opposite the entrance to Kinburn House and in the same style, inhabited in the past by Maitlands and Jacksons.

In January 1905, Violet Martin, the Ross of 'Somerville and Ross', stayed in Kinburn West with the Jacksons. She arrived in a poorish state, bruised and travel weary. However, she found Kinburn West, and indeed St Andrews itself, delightful 'It is a cultured place and all the new books are here . . . It is a semi-detached suburban house most comfortable and roomy and has lovely Chip and Sheraton things in the drawing room and old silver. My bed is luxurious, ditto my bath and the food is excellent.' Early in her visit she went to dine with the Langs where she met among others Principal Donaldson and some Everards. She and Andrew Lang took an instant shine to each other; she describes him as 'very curious to look at – tall, very thin, white hair growing far down his forehead and shading dark eye-brows and piercing-looking charming brown eyes. He has a somewhat foxy profile, a lemon pale face and a black moustache. I think he is shy. [He] exhibited at intervals a curious silent laugh, up under his nose. He will be very nut-crackery as an old man.'

Violet Martin went on a round of dissipation in St Andrews. *The Real Charlotte* had just been published and she found many of her new acquaintances had read it and were full of its praise including 'a very clever woman who wears a false nose.' After dinner one night Mr Jackson showed some slides which Miss

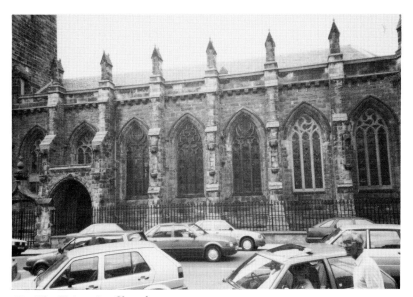

47   The University Church

48   The ruins of the East End of the cathedral and St Rule's Tower, 1880

49 The author at St Mary's College

50 Jessie Anderson, the family nurse, with the author's sisters Gwyn and Nancie

51 The author's son Andrew in Abbotsford Crescent during the Second World War. Notice the mounting blocks

52   The Lammas Fair

53   Dancing at the Lammas Fair about the turn of the century

54 Dr Moir, founder of St Andrews Cottage Hospital, and his family in Abbey Walk near St Leonard's

55 Students taking their Sunday morning walk on the pier after church

56 Winston Churchill inspecting the St Andrews defences during the Second World War. The defence of St Andrews was in the charge of a Polish contingent

57 James Chisholm, the newspaper seller whose 'cry' mingled with the church bells as he drove around the town on Sunday mornings

58　John Paton

59　Alan Boase, with his sister Sylvia, who died of meningitis contracted while at boarding school. Sylvia is holding John Paton

60　Dr Paton

61　Sir Hugh Lyon Playfair, *c.* 1855

62 Lord Lyon Playfair, *c*. 1860, the chicken stealer

63 Professor John Burnet, St Andrews University, *c*. 1900. A good profile for a professor of Greek

64 The east end of North Street recalls a time when fishing was a busy industry in St Andrews

65   North Street, 1891

66   'Joan'. Mrs Henry Clarke,
the best-known of St Andrews
fishwives,   in   her   working
clothes

67   Forgan the club-maker

Martin described as very good but Andrew Lang took a scunner at them and sulked in the next room, an example of his affected poses, the sort of thing which no doubt annoyed Max Beerbohm who detested him. Miss Martin shrieked like a dog, which bewildered and perturbed but did not amuse Lang. 'He asked me in an unhappy way how I did it. I said, "By main strength, the way the man played the fiddle."'

Lang offered to show her St Andrews and, having failed to turn up on two fine days, arrived at Kinburn West in a blizzard. However, they set off: 'You will observe that I was keeping my tail very erect. In the iron blast we went down South Street. It is a little like the High at Oxford on a small trimmed scale.' I do not see the resemblance; South Street, or at least the east end of it, resembles nothing very closely but itself. However, if comparisons must be made, it seems to me more like a French provincial street than the English Oxford High Street. After spending another day with him in Edinburgh, Violet Martin wrote, 'Lastly I may remark that when he leaves St Andrews tomorrow all other men go with him – as far as I am concerned – or rather they stay and they seem bourgeois and commonplace – all except my nice Mr Jackson.' She did not find all St Andrews' figures so sympathetic. 'I hated Professor Knight . . . his breath was pestilence and his conversation purely perfunctory.' However, on the whole her visit went well.

At No. 2 Kinburn Place lives Ronald Cant, one of the most distinguished scholars who has never become a professor, a fount of knowledge about St Andrews and more than that. He is a survivor of the great university tradition, the tradition of Newman and the civilization descended from Greece. Ronald is one of the few people I have met who is oblivious to prestige. He could easily have become a professor. He could have climbed the ladder of academic career structures. He could have written voluminous books. Instead he published a number of short, concise essays (such as his history of the university). They are distinguished in themselves and distinguished among modern academic/bureaucratic literature by their readability, their accuracy, their conciseness and their lack of pointless footnotes and quotations. Generations of St Andrews' students and others have benefited by his teaching. As well as all this, he is a very nice man and an excellent gossip.

Turning north-west from Cants' house, we go up Kennedy Gardens. These are called, I suppose, after the Bishop Kennedy who founded St Salvator's College, whose tomb in the university's church was desecrated by the barbarian reformers and whose 'niece' still presides over the annual student revels. In a house on the left lived the Cunningham family. Sir George, who had been a civil servant in India, was nominally retired but exceptionally active and merry, as were his sister and brother. He was representative of another coterie in the St Andrews of my day, the prosperous retired. If you penetrate into the Big Room in the Royal and Ancient you will find comfortable leather furniture, all provided or at least refurbished by his brother.

When it reaches the escarpment which used to bound Rathelpie to the north, Kennedy Gardens takes a sharply angled bend to the left. To the right, following the wall of Kinburn House, leads a path, known as Jacob's Ladder, which turns north-west down the hill. The field in its angle, now occupied by a university building, at one time played an important part in the winter life of St Andrews, for on it tobogganing took place and near its foot where it joins the Guardbridge road in a ruff of black fir trees lay a curling pond. Somewhere here at the top of Jacob's Ladder stood the windmill which was approached from the north by Windmill Road.

Now go back round the corner. On the north side in Kennedy Gardens was the gate leading to Westerlea, of which

Milne was the architect. It would have been a startling house even at the head of some Highland loch: as a suburban villa with its tower and battlements it passed all reason. It belonged to the Wilsons, rather a large and talented family. Mr Wilson, no doubt untruly, was said to have been so rich that he invested his annual income and lived on the dividends. Anyway, he lived pretty well. The inside of his house was, as might be expected, cavernous. Children's parties were interrupted after dark by a footman who not only drew the curtains but, if my recollection is reliable, covered the stags' heads which decorated the walls with white covers for the night. Can this really have been so? If not, why have I invented it? Of the daughters, Hilda was a notable golfer and Doris an ornithologist. I spent many happy hours with her on the rocks watching ducks and gulls.

On the opposite side of the road stand two more houses in the baronial style – Rathmore and Afton – the latter also designed by Milne, built for Aikman the grocer, but taken over by the Everard family along with Rathmore. Why the Everards required two such inconvenient houses next door to each other I cannot guess. They were another well-known St Andrews family, one of whom wrote a history of the Royal and Ancient Club. Eda Everard was my godmother: she lived with her sister Madeleine at Rathmore. Rathmore is imprinted on my memory as the typical Victorian house, a suitable setting for innumerable scenes from the Brontës to Landseer. Its rooms contrived to be both lofty and gloomy.

Eda suffered ill-health vaguely connected with her heart. This Victorian condition had nothing dramatic about it; it was not connected with imminent death. A Miss Sharp of a slightly earlier generation had gone to bed in her twenties and never 'got up' again. She lived into her eighties, apparently happily. Eda, in spite of her bad health, was an excellent godmother. Nevertheless, however much some invalids may have 'enjoyed' their ill-health, it spread a sort of sweet fog around their houses. The pot-pourris, the half-drawn blinds and the heavy side-boards imposed a hush. It was the only house in which I constantly saw a chaise longue used for its proper purpose. Eda was usually recumbent upon it. Though the drawing room on the first floor was the centre of such St Andrews houses, it was the entrance hall which made the most lasting impression on children. In them children removed their snow-shoes and their shawls were removed by nanny. The hall tables each had a bowl full of visiting cards, the inner door was glazed with coloured glass and the atmosphere was staid.

Later at Rathmore lived Mrs Hotchkiss, daughter of Mr Ionides, a patron and collector. Some of the contents of her home, such as her sideboard, are now in the Victorian collection in the Victoria and Albert Museum. In my youth her brother-in-law was a solicitor in St Andrews. He shared a shoot with Dr Paton. Mr Hotchkiss was a taciturn man with cropped hair and a leathery skin. He arrived at the shoot in an open car beside which he would sometimes, if it was a fine day, walk with one hand on the steering wheel and hand throttle. However fine the day he wore two mackintoshes. (Teddy Lee, another frequent participant at these shoots, says he wore three but this, I think, he exaggerates.) These mackintoshes had to be taken off and put on again at every fence, which somewhat delayed us. According to his nephew, 'My uncle was not a sociable type – his great interest was wars. He dropped his practice to go to the Boer War. He did the same in the Great War even though he was fifty-one. He was annoyed that they would not take him even in the Home Guard in the Second World War.' He was by then nearly eighty. He ordered his clothes from Harrods, simply telling them to send 'the same again' when they were worn out. As he liked everything three sizes too big, fit was unimportant.

Walking further along Kennedy Gardens we come to University Hall, again by Gillespie and Scott. This was the earliest hall of residence built for the first women students. Like a bird prospecting for new fields to visit it was the precursor of those laboratories which now have engulfed what was a rural slope overlooking the fields of Strathtyrum. In the house called Westoun opposite University Hall lived Peter Graham RA, a reproduction of whose picture of Highland cattle, as I have noted, hung in our spare bedroom at 8 Abbotsford Crescent. After him, Ned Boase, brother of Philip and Norman, lived in the house. The Boases, for all their enterprise in business and immersion in local affairs, led in some ways a curiously withdrawn life. Ned's son married Lydia Mayne, a St Andrews beauty. On meeting her out pushing a pram one day they were delighted to find that it contained their grandchild, already several months old, whom they had not seen before.

The first article I wrote (published in the *St Andrews Citizen*) was a protest against ubiquitous green belts and in favour of the green fingers of the country reaching into town, as these fields and the Ladebraes walk did at St Andrews – rather a good variation on conventional town planning. I still think ribbon development has its successes and Hepburn Gardens, or 'out the road' as it was known, is one of them. To it we now return by way of Donaldson Gardens, named after the estimable principal who raised St Andrews to the top of the British university tree after Oxford and Cambridge. He also paid, or arranged for the payment of, Professor Burnet's debts. Where Donaldson Gardens meet Hepburn Gardens you will see St Leonard's Church, a good, modest building rather like the Catholic church on the Scores which it pre-dates, and even more like the Town Church which was restored by its architect, Macgregor Chalmers of Glasgow. It was completed in 1904. It is a parish church but the parish is peculiar. It consists of bits of land isolated from one another, united only by having at one time belonged to St Leonard's College. After St Leonard's College was amalgamated with St Salvator's the parish congregation, which had previously worshipped in St Leonard's Chapel, moved to what is now the University Church – an inconvenient arrangement, for St Salvator's Church was hardly big enough to cater for the whole university, let alone a parish congregation as well. The present building is a nice plain church in the Norman manner.

Here I recommend going back a hundred yards or so towards the town to glance at the houses on the south side of Hepburn Gardens. They are by the ubiquitous and chameleon-like Gillespie and Scott, this time in an early twentieth-century art nouveau suburban style with red roofs, iron balconies and white stucco – about as far from the Scottish baronial Gothic as you can get. My mother lived in No. 22 after she left Abbotsford Crescent; they were pleasant, airy houses with big windows looking over the Ladebraes.

Going westward again you pass what used to be Mabel Boase's stables. She hunted regularly and wrote some essays on horses and riding. A tall, straight-backed lady with a handsome oval face, she looked well on a side-saddle. Mrs Boase's summer outfit consisted of a white fur hat, thick white stockings, white buckskin shoes and a white-striped dress – like the old Kodak girl. (I am indebted to John Paton's widow for prodding my memory about this.) Once she had assumed this plumage, like a guillemot she wore it until autumn. Further along on the south side, just at the fork of the road, a drive leads off to another university hall of residence called after Prior Hepburn. The road forks here, the right fork leading to Strathkinness, Ceres and eventually Kirkcaldy. On the right you pass the university's playing fields, the observatory and a new hall of residence named after Sir David Russell, who

restored St Leonard's Chapel which we will see later. The left
fork, which was once the road to the Forth ferries, now has a
new housing estate at the end before you reach Mount Melville
but carries little except local traffic.

On the Mount Melville road, however, stand several of the
largest of the St Andrews villas of post-Westerlea vintage. The
first of these next to Hepburn Hall is the White House, the
home in my time of Norman and Mabel Boase. Norman was a
flax spinner at the Boase spinning company of Leven and
Dundee, a Provost of St Andrews and a figure in the Royal and
Ancient. Among the leading families of St Andrews the Boases
might be said to have taken over from the Playfairs. They
illustrated the shift of prestige from the academic and professional families, often with members in the Church and politics,
to commercial leaders. The change was not immediate nor
complete, indeed the two sets of dignitaries had many ideas in
common and shared similar abilities and values. But they did
not confuse these values. The new leaders served, for instance,
on university courts, but did not believe that commercial
success was the only test of education or that universities
existed solely to train men, far less women, for industry. The
Boases were a family with strong intellects woven into which,
like a bright streak in a sober tartan, was aesthetic appreciation
and a certain liking for instructing others – qualities they turned
to good effect. Norman's son, Alan, ended up as Professor of
French in Glasgow and their cousin, Tom, from Dundee,
became Director of the Courtauld Institute and President of
Magdalen College, Oxford.

Boase does not sound like a Scottish name. I associate it with
Sandeman, another clever family in eastern Scotland, who were
also in the textile trade – Sandeman's Cotton Belting of Stanley
on the Tay. As far as I know no Sandeman lived in the city of
St Andrews but Sir Nairn, an MP, lived at Kenly Green in the

parish. The Sandemans are said to have come from Cornwall, founding their own church in Scotland. Faraday, the scientist, was a member of it. Perhaps the Boases also came from south-west England. Their abilities seem to have broken out again in commercial activities. Alan's son is an advertising magnate. Alan's sister, Sylvia should not be forgotten, though, alas, she died very young. She was one of my young loves.

Further along from the White House, Wayside stands bang on the road. It is by Lorimer in his English style. Like the Hill of Tarvit near Ceres it is one of the most inhabitable of his houses, with all the finish which makes Lorimer houses distinctive. I believe him to have been one of Britain's best architects. A Lorimer house, though usually inconvenient and quirky, draws one to it. Like the yak it is an attractive beast especially for children. Poke behind Wayside and you will find yet another Gillespie and Scott house not, as I write, quite finished and in yet another style – a sober variety of the Scottish tradition with only one round tower. Wayside belonged to the abundant family of Crawford, who had numerous daughters and two sons, one of whom still farms at Naughton not far away.

Beyond Wayside are several large houses, one distinguished by a concave front and another, Balnacarron, in times past by a family of stone owls which sat upon its wall – delightful birds after whom, in my family, the owner was called Mrs 'Owls' Boothby to distinguish her from other Boothbys. Her daughter Betty Boothby, was an admired figure, riding a motorbike and being a very good golfer. Balnacarron was later the home of the Hows. And so we come to the last house – Lawpark. Shortly before you reach Lawpark stands the stone which marks the first mile from St Andrews. Few of these triangular milestones with their elegant abbreviations of place names still exist. This one shows Burntisland – which would have been the ferry terminal for Edinburgh – 29 miles, Ceres 6 miles and Cupar 8 miles. Lawpark was a most important and delightful bit of St Andrews where Norman's brother, Philip Boase, and his wife, Bessie, lived. They had no children but Philip made up for it by being like the best of children himself. His main enthusiasm was fish. He had dug at the bottom of the garden a pond, perhaps 20 by 10 yards and a dozen feet deep. In this he kept tremendous brown and rainbow trout, up to and exceeding 10 lbs. For children these provided magical treats, of which three were especially memorable. At the side of the pond was a cellar with a window from which you could watch these giant fish lazily wallowing or ogling against the glass. Then you could dance a reed with a mussel on the end about 6 in above the surface of the pond and experience the shock of a trout erupting to seize it with a breathtaking splash. And when the pond was drained for cleaning you might be invited to see men in waders catching the fish in nets as they flopped about in the receding water.

The attractions of the Boases for a boy were not confined to fish. Bessie was a keen gardener who bent with industry over her borders, often accompanied by advice – but not much physical assistance – from Douglas Young. Douglas Young lived near St Fort. He was tall, thin and bearded. A genuine scholar, being for a time a university lecturer in the Classics, he was also a mine of inaccurate information. He was speculative and dogmatic about the results of his speculation. He enjoyed argument. In fact, he resembled many Scots, though not as combative as some. When I visited Shetland with him he stopped outside the Mission to Fishermen in Lerwick to draw my attention to a faded notice which, among other services offered to fishermen, listed 'Hand Dressing'. 'That is most interesting Jo,' he pronounced. 'It goes back to the days when fishermen could not write so the Mission provided letter writers for them.' The notice meant what it said – that if fishermen or fisher-lassies with their gutting knives cut their hands, as they often did, they could get the cuts dressed at the Mission.

Walter Elliot reminded me of him in mind, if not in body. Walter assured me with didactic certainty that poplars would not grow north of Inverness. I planted six and they grew no worse than any other trees in Orkney. Douglas always appeared pleased to see people and apparently was certain that they would be pleased to see him. He also had excellent manners. The hearts of such as my mother who otherwise would have shied at his pre-Raphaelite or Tennysonian appearance with wide-brimmed hat and tweed trousers and who disapproved of some of his opinions (he was a voluble Scottish Nationalist), were softened by his agreeability. Foibles which might have been met with derision, such as publishing in 'Lallans' a slim volume *Frae the Bulgarian* though he did not speak a word of that language, were passed off with smiles. Alas, his beard itself was not a foible: as a haemophiliac he could not shave and died young.

The other entertainments provided by Philip Boase lay around Leuchars. The wide fields of oats and potatoes provided excellent feed for partridges, which nested in great numbers in the long grass surrounding the tiny fir trees which the Forestry Commission were planting on part of Tent's Muir. There during the Christmas holidays Philip would muster the St Andrews boys such as myself, the Patons and Teddy Lee, accompanied by some of their parents. 'Padre' Wilson, Teddy's stepfather, was a deadly shot who engendered as much enthusiasm as Philip himself. Common tactics were for a line of guns to start off in single file between the fields and the plantations. When the leader of this file was 150 to 200 yards ahead, Philip, with some other guns and beaters, would advance at right-angles through the fields. That no one was killed was a tribute to the restraint with which Philip, the 'Padre' and Dr Paton managed to temper the general enthusiasm. Philip Boase, with his round, eager face rather like a fish, had the unworldly, benevolent quality of the Boases. As well as boys he entertained tramps, whom he fed on tea-cake.

Back in St Andrews we have now reached what used to be the end of the town. Lawpark and a house belonging to another family of textile spinners, the Piries, on the opposite side of the road mark the place where the road to Mount Melville crosses the Kinness burn. True, further up the burn stood Carron Lodge where a retired Colonel Sutherland and his family lived in a low house crouched in the valley. Later Mrs Gilroy of a family of jute weavers built Rufflets, now an hotel.

A graveyard, a primary school and a housing estate have extended the town to the West. I suppose we should be grateful that the planners have not torn down the centre of the city to built the large factory-like schools that modern education seems to demand. But if you cut the schools off from the houses and the shops you tear something of its heart from the community. Further, I am not sure that characterless schools with huge windows, polythene, gravel and uninviting corridors add much to education, however hygienic they may be. They may indeed detract from it, making it a soul-less curriculum-grinding process. My first experience of Eton was a house which any modern sanitary inspector would certainly condemn and a classroom which was originally, I imagine, a Tudor cellar with ink-spattered, name-carved desks: unpretentious but cosy. Passing the old primary school off Greyfriars Gardens during school breaks was like skirting a fairground; a merry noise bounced off the douce houses of the St Andrews bourgeoisie and small coteries of boys and girls seemed for ever buzzing around like starlings and, like starlings, suddenly perching on some convenient wall.

However, it is time to turn towards home. Going down to the Ladebraes burn, where the road crosses it you find one of the most delectable places on earth. Overhung with trees the burn rambles away to the east. Across a stone bridge stands the remains of a mill and its pond, the path flush with the water. It is, and has been all my life, inhabited by the greediest of ducks. They swim in a pack to greet every new visitor, quacking on the bank demanding food. Never as a child did my nurse and I go for a walk to the end of the Ladebraes without a parcel of stale bread. Nowhere does water gurgle more soothingly up to, even over, the banks of paths. Nowhere does spring with daffodils (planted by Philip Boase) flower more freshly under the dappled shadows of the budding trees.

All the way back to St Andrews the path winds above the burn with diversions to the water's edge or up to the mouldering fence of the Hepburn Gardens houses above it. Indeed, between these fences and the trees and bushes on the main path lie other paths passable only by children. Another old mill lies half way to St Andrews. The old mills of the parish are described in an excellent article written by Mr Smart and published by the St Andrews Preservation Trust. The country part of the Ladebraes walk comes to an end at the west end of the 'Argyle suburb', as it is rather grandly described in the First Statistical Account of 1793. According to this Account, which is full of information, the number of souls in the parishes of St Andrews and St Leonards was 3,950, of which 2,390 lived in St Andrews, 129 in the suburb of Argyle and 1,431 in the country. A weighbridge stands at the junction of the way up from the Ladebraes and the wall carries a strict injunction against bicycling. St Andrews and the bicycle were locked in mutual necessity and suspicion. The bicycle was a main means of travel but, for that reason I suppose, was jealously repelled from pedestrian areas.

Rejoining the road, the first turning on the right leads back to the Braes past a charming row of cottages with gardens in front of them where Lydia Mayne lived. Then you come to the remains of Stewart's cleck works where irons with his pipe trademark were made, and so to the rather distinguished building of the Whey-Pat. On the other side of the road grouped round a yard stood the Argyle Brewery with red pantiles, then degenerated to the manufacture of fizzy drinks but still a notable feature until the war. Milne the architect lived at 34 Argyle Street. Finally on this side of the road stands the Gibson Hospital, designed by Henry as a home for old folks built and endowed by the Gibson family.

If instead of going up to the junction of Hepburn Gardens and Argyle Street you kept along the path, you would come to the semi-detached villa, Laurel Bank, in which one of my aunts lodged in a household typical of the St Andrews of her time. The house belonged to Mary Munro who kept it, like herself, as bright as a button. Constant housework and cooking seemed to make her as rosy as an apple though, except to work with my aunt in the tiny garden or to shop in the town, I never saw her go out. My aunt lived in the front room and was, alas, very deaf. The third occupant was Mrs Cunningham, whose position was slightly ambivalent. She ordinarily wore a lace cap and an apron and was to be found, a comfortable figure, in the kitchen. What happened to her when Mary and my aunt went on holiday I am not sure. The holiday now seems rather remarkable for it consisted of picking raspberries at Blairgowrie, where they took a house. Raspberry pickers were often tinkers and such-like casual workers, not always of the highest respectability. My aunt and Mary, though poor, were extremely respectable. As I have said, there were many similar landladies in St Andrews catering for retired people, usually single, or for students and visitors.

My aunt came to lunch every Sunday. After lunch she and I, picking up the dogs belonging to another aunt, went for a walk. None of my aunts had any interest in golf. Though the obvious place for a Sunday walk was the links I seldom remember going there. Instead we went up the Ladebraes, or took the road to the south or, most frequently of all, walked along the East Cliffs beyond the harbour. Though small, St Andrews had clearly marked social groups and territories: the university; the fishermen or their descendants from whom the caddies were largely recruited; the visitors of the upper stratum who came for golf and often spent a month or more in the town; the shopkeepers; the merchants, some of whom, including my father and uncle, commuted to Dundee or even Edinburgh; and the holiday trippers.

The South and
St Leonards

Starting south from the town hall, I never find Queens Gardens as nice as it should be. Its houses are all right, and it has harboured several interesting people – Edwin Muir for a time lived at No. 20 and Professor Burnet at No. 19. I like the arrangement of gardens across the street. It should be as attractive as Greyfriars Gardens – its double – but somehow it isn't. The gardens, with some notable exceptions, such as those of Nos 10 and 16 kept, respectively, by Mrs Moffet and by Mrs Rose, both daughters of Padre Wilson, which are in immaculate order and gorgeous bloom, look a little neglected and to me shops lend interest to a street. At the foot on the left we find a large building, St Regulus, designed by Rae in a baronial style – not however specifically Scots. It was here St Leonard's Girls' School started. Rae indeed laid out Queens Gardens and designed several of the sober villas in it. On the right is a large Episcopal church of which Rowan Anderson was the architect. Up until the war it had a tower which has now been taken down. I am always surprised that St Andrews supports two Episcopal congregations in these Godless days – for that we must largely thank the Younger generosity to All Saints.

Queens Terrace, which crosses the 'T' at the end of Queens

Gardens, comes to an abrupt end where the Ladebraes walk runs across it on its way into South Street. In this terrace, for a time after moving from Hepburn Gardens, lived Dr Brink, afterwards Professor of Latin at Cambridge; so did the Skenes and, in the rectory, the Price family. Over the wall you may see the second or third ugliest building in St Andrews, a typical out–of–scale matchbox, luckily concealed from most angles. Like its rival for bad architecture, the new Student Union, it is a child of the university. Just up to the right off the path which leads to South Street is a backwater of houses in which it must be pleasant and convenient to live.

Turning to the left along the Ladebraes you pass a large house called Netherton. I should like to know who built it and why. Carrying on to the west across Bridge Street, passing my aunt's house, Laurel Bank, you will come to a path leading south. It follows the old railway line. Though monotonously bordered by a hedge of macrocarpa, it makes a pleasant addition to St Andrews' walks. Turning right at the end you can go into the Botanic Gardens. These originally belonged to the university. The old Botanic Gardens behind St Mary's College having been built over, new gardens were made south of the Ladebraes and west of the line of the old railway. The university, however, found that it could not afford their upkeep so the District Council took them on. They are a pleasant place in which to sit, calm and uncrowded. When I was last there on a fine Sunday in July I saw only six other people. Many of the flowers being familiar, the atmosphere is friendly rather than exotic; perhaps a 'farm park' might be added. Such a 'park' has proved popular in Orkney, peopled by more or less familiar breeds of cattle, sheep and pigs, as well as several varieties of ducks and hens, among which children can roam. Better still some benefactor might re-create Provost Playfair's garden which (following Helen Cook) I will describe later in this walk.

However, to return to the banks of the town. I find the bank facing south one of the most agreeable parts of St Andrews. I believe that some of the earliest religious foundations settled at the east end of this district of Kilrymont. The people who settled there were wise. I suppose that the needs of defence and prestige drove them up the hill. But why was this district ignored in the building boom of the nineteenth century? Why perch looking north on the windswept Scores when you could bask on the southern face of the hill among gardens? Golf and 'the view' are, I suppose, the answers. At the foot of a path which we passed earlier on in this walk lie in a quiet corner of the burn some older cottages dating from the eighteenth century. These have a countrified air and no doubt at one time had small farms attached to them. My aunt from Laurel Bank ended her days here in Nelson Street but the neighbourhood has changed out of recognition.

Even before the Second World War new houses had begun to creep out of the Largo road, obliterating the farms and woodland at Kilrymont. Beyond them lies the inevitable 'industrial estate' of garages and such-like. I do not know the history of planning. As I have mentioned, old St Andrews is admirably 'planned' to lead up to the cathedral, but whether there was ever any 'plan' seems doubtful. Now we have many planning departments with large staffs, but 'new' St Andrews seems to be a haphazard web of streets and squares without any focal points. I suspect that good architecture makes good planning. The architects of the last seventy years have, on the whole, been poor. Nevertheless there are some comfortable-looking houses in the district. The gardens in general are better kept than most of Queens Gardens and there is an attractive group of, presumably, more expensive houses further to the east. The lack of shops or industry makes zoning, so beloved by local planners, dull.

Travelling along the south bank of the Ladebraes or Kinness burn, I am glad to see that there are plenty of ducks rather less voracious than their cousins up stream. Recently one was good enough to lay an egg as I watched her. In a garden on the east side of the path leading up to Queens Terrace there lived an owl in a commodious and shady cage. I nearly described it as a tame owl, but the experience of trying to help an ostensibly injured owl in Orkney which malingered for weeks, feasting on prime liver and biting everyone who fed it, makes me think that no owls are ever tame. They are savage though sagacious birds who exploit any human that they can seduce into looking after them. It was in this house, once inhabited by the acolytes of this sagacious bird, that the equally sagacious and much more friendly Professor Brink lived.

Across the burn from Kinness Burn Road, on which we are walking, is a row of small villas called Dempster Terrace. If I were ever to retire to St Andrews it would be to Dempster Terrace – if I were lucky enough to find a house there. There used to be a tennis club at Kilrymont with two or three hard courts which, when flooded during hard frosts, became skating rinks. The only feature I can now find which may be their successor is a bowling green. I do not know whether Dempster Terrace was named after a particular Dempster or after the family in general. They were long a prominent St Andrews family, or families. I am not clear that they were all related. They pre-dated the Playfairs, coming from the same part of the world – Angus. We have already met them in connection with rabbits on the links.

George Dempster was the most widely known Dempster. He was born in 1732 and inherited the property of Dunniden in Angus. In 1760 he was chosen as Provost of St Andrews, remaining in office until 1776. However, as he was also the Member of Parliament for the Perth boroughs (which included

St Andrews), he presumably did not do much work in the town. In 1811 he bought a house in South Street 'for the sake of spending the winter near a public library and a game of whist'. Public library? I never knew there were public libraries in Scotland before Carnegie. From then on he spent some months every year in South Street sending round a coach to collect the old ladies for his whist parties. Whist and Bridge have long been almost as much played in St Andrews as golf. He was a member of the brilliant Edinburgh society of the late eighteenth century. Those who want to know more of Scottish society and the background of Scottish politics of those days, as well as being entertained, should read his letters to Sir Adam Fergusson, admirably edited by the descendant of the latter, Sir James Fergusson.

George Dempster was one of the improving landlords of his time. He also made great efforts, particularly through the Fisheries Society, to help the Highlanders (he acquired the estate of Skibo near Tain, afterwards owned by Carnegie). Too little credit has been given to such as he for their exertions after the '45. Highland development, even to the founding of new towns, is not a new activity. He encouraged the flax industry and was the first to suggest the transport of fish in ice (which he learnt from the Chinese). He spoke Icelandic, was a friend of the Icelandic sage, Thorkelin (who got an honorary degree at St Andrews University), travelled the Continent, held sensible views on education and supported the right political causes – including the freedom of the American colonies.

Though he deplored Highland dress and the bagpipes he 'attacked the feudal dragon in his den who of his slaves made valiant Highland Men. In vain I tried the Highlanders to keep from being devoured by flocks of Lowland sheep.' He tossed off a good deal of verse, among which I rather like the sentimental epitaph on his nephew's canary (having no children

he and his wife looked after this boy whose mother died of
consumption and whose father was drowned – the nephew
himself died at the age of five):

> Farewell, poor Jacky once the joy and care
> Of little George, my darling and my heir.
> Fate snatched my boy; kind Rosy [his wife] took the cage
> Saw Jacky die in good old age.
> His days were blythe, tho' undiversified;
> He lived in plenty and in peace he died.
> To Heaven I hope his harmless soul is flown,
> His body's buried underneath this stone.

The medallion by James Tassie shows a well-looking Rae-
burnesque figure with prominent nose and eyes. His portrait in
old age is somewhat sadder. He must have been an exceptionally nice man.

Cathcart Dempster, a native St Andrean described as a
'gentleman of talent', was his younger near contemporary. He
for many years was the leading spirit on the Town Council, for
the Earl of Kellie, then the provost, seldom turned up. He did
much for the town, improving the harbour and acquiring the
site for the present town hall. He claimed to be the discoverer of
Ryan's Patent Antiseptic and raised much money for the poor.

If you care to make a diversion here you can climb Greenside
Place to rest on a bench under the abbey wall. You can then
contemplate once again the change of architecture. Compare
the simple house opposite with its sedate and modest air and a
little beauty with the fidgety and pretentious building on the
corner of Abbey Street. From here the most obvious way to the
harbour is down Abbey Walk along the priory wall and past the
Teinds Gate. If you take this route you will see the Cottage
Hospital on your right, which was founded by Dr Moir. As an

alternative, you may find it more adventurous to go down the hill again and, after re-crossing the burn, continue east. On the right, nearly opposite the bridge which leads to Greenside Place, is a curious brick building – the Boys' Brigade Hall. It is a relic of the days when the land beyond the burn was a recreational fringe of the town. Then you pass into a neglected part of the town. The burn, which is here fenced off, runs through a wilderness. There is a rather dour open space flanked to the South by more modern housing and to the east by a few Edwardian houses through which you reach the coast road to Kingsbarn and Crail. To your left, below the bridge on which the road crosses the burn, once lived the great Professor Burnet. He was Professor of Greek. He wrote the best book on education, *Secondary Education in Germany*, that I have ever read. He was also given to drinking.

On the seaward side you find the East Sands running from the harbour to the East Cliffs. Were they not so vastly outstripped by the magnificent West Sands they would be quite a notable stretch of sand in their own right. They were too far away for any but special expeditions for children who lived in Abbotsford Crescent (or as the beginning of cliff walks with my aunt's dogs), but onto their shore looked three interesting buildings: a rather formidable factory-like building with a squat chimney, which seems always to have been derelict. This was originally the depot of Gibsons who were timber importers, the same family who founded the Gibson Hospital near the West Port; the Gatty marine laboratory, over which our landlord Professor McIntosh, with his white beard, presided, and the Woodburn Steam Laundry. Before the days of laundrettes and washing machines the Woodburn Laundry, like the railway station before buses and cars, played a considerable part in St Andrews' life. It was not a meeting place like the station but its baskets were met in every middle-class home. It was managed for a short time in the '90s by Sir Edward Playfair's mother, who acted as a substitute for the regular manageress who was ill. One customer regularly sent in horribly dirty pants. Mrs Playfair asked the tough old fisherwoman if she minded handling them. 'Oh no,' she replied, 'He's some mother's child.' Near it the lifeboat lived after it ceased to be launched across the West Sands.

Up the hill towards Kingsbarns you will see a strange cantonment of caravans. There is nothing to be done about this except to use your imagination and pretend that either they are Pictish villages or the tents of an invading army. In any case, they are not permanent and perhaps one day the ground will be returned to farming as it was when it formed the country estate of the well-known family of Grace. Though the Graces owned a house which must have been not much more than half a mile outside the town, they kept a townhouse in South Street to which they retreated in winter. The Grace family were the leading St Andrews solicitors. Now this firm is part of an amalgamation which stretches to Cupar and employs ten partners. In the last century Charles Grace was also the unpaid Secretary of the Royal and Ancient Club for forty years. I doubt if he even charged expenses. Today there are some twenty secretaries employed by the club. Until recently the banks in small towns were often run by local solicitors. The Graces presided over the Royal Bank of Scotland in Market Street.

If you turn back across the outer side of the harbour you get a view of the cathedral and its surroundings which must have been magnificent. Nowadays it is difficult to visualize the harbour as it was in its days of greatness. According to the Second Statistical Account the Spring Fair was descibed as 'The renowned faire of St Andrews, called the Senzie Mercat held and kept for fifteen days and beginning the second week after Easter whereen to resorted merchants from most of the then trading kingdomes in Europe: trade in the kingdome being then in its infancie.' 'At this period,' the Second Statistical Account goes on, 'according to tradition from 200 to 300 vessels have been seen in the bay and harbour of St Andrews.' But by the time this Statistical Account was written (1838) the Fair had dwindled away and occupied only a single day.

We cross the bridge between the inner and outer harbours, avert our eyes from the building which now looks over the outer harbour and pass through the gateway in Prior Hepburn's wall into the Pends. It seems to be a favourite fly-catching pitch for swallows and swifts. Whether the Swallowgate which stood on the Scores near the cathedral had anything to do with these birds I cannot tell for certain but, I believe scholars say that it does not. Why should they say this? Personally I associate such birds with medieval gateways. This gateway used to be wrapped in a distinctive smell of gas and seaweed. With the closing of the gas works the gas element has departed from the smell, but the seaweed remains.

On our right is the graveyard which we have already visited. On the left, going up the Pends, have stood various buildings associated over the years with St Andrews and its better-known inhabitants. Here in comparatively recent times lived Bishop Wordsworth, a member of that family of argumentative and overbearing though erudite academics who produced at least three bishops but were no relation to the poet, whom we met on the Scores, and Dr Chalmers, who led the Great Secession from the established Church of Scotland. Long before their day, and further up the road, stood the palace, the Novum Hospitium, in which James V hoped to settle his charming but delicate Queen Madeleine from France. For a time, spring seemed to have broken out in Scotland after the winter of Flodden. James was a prince of the Renaissance who encouraged learning and civilized amusements, but sadly Madeleine died. Her successor,

Mary of Guise, visited the palace. It has entirely disappeared, although a gateway, altered and on a new site, remains.

Before the Novum Hospitium there was already a medieval hospice off the Pends kept by the monks of the priory for the benefit of pilgrims. Its site and some remains of its buildings are incorporated in St Leonard's School.

I don't know why the school was dedicated to St Leonard, as he seems to have had no connection with St Andrews and spent most of his life in a forest in Limousin. However, he has left his name imprinted on the town. With the end of the Middle Ages 'the desire for pilgrims cooled', as the author of the Second Statistical Account puts it. He continues:

> An experiment was accordingly made to convert it [the Hospice] into a hospital or nunnery for the reception of females considerably advanced in years who might there devote themselves to the performance of religious duties; but it failed to realize the expectations which had been formed of its utility, its inmates having exhibited no indications of a regard for either morality or piety.

So in 1512 Prior Hepburn diverted its buildings and revenues to found St Leonard's College. This college survived until 1747 when it was amalgamated with St Salvator's. In the middle of the last century Principal Forbes attempted something of a revival of St Leonard's College by lodging some twenty boys in the surviving buildings, hoping no doubt that it would grow into a fully-fledged college. Andrew Lang, who was one of the inmates, much enjoyed it. But after a year or two it had to be closed. By that time the college system had become supposedly alien to Scottish universities. However, I believe that the school house which confronts you as you enter from the Pends retains some of the original buildings going back at least to St

Leonard's College. What is undoubtedly true is that the college chapel survives on your right. After years of neglect it has been excellently restored, largely with money provided by Sir David Russell, a paper-maker, who served for many years on the University Court. I am glad to know that he got some of the stones to repave the nave from the back garden of 8 Abbotsford Crescent.

From the Pends the school is approached by a short avenue branching off to the left. Alas, this is now another municipal blot on the city. It is the scene of one or two of the ghost stories of Mr Linskill, the historian of St Andrews' ghosts, and in my youth the Dean of Guild or chief planner of the city. He was a good enough golfer to be commended for his putting in the *Badminton Book of Golf*. A convivial man, he once delighted my extremely proper aunt, Miss Gordon, who enquired why his thumb was bandaged by replying that he had trodden on it going home the previous evening. He had two other claims to fame: he disrupted the traffic in North Street by several 'digs' intended to discover a secret passage between the castle and the cathedral; and he is also said to have travelled on the train which went to the bottom in the Tay Bridge disaster, but to have left it at St Fort, the last station before Dundee, because he did not like the weather. He introduced golf to Cambridge and Oxford, being the first President of the Cambridge University Golf Club. The ghosts who haunted this little avenue included a phantom coach and coachman, and a lady who had slit his lips and nostrils to fend off marriage to a repugnant suitor being forced on her by her parents. The avenue used to be suitably dank and forlorn, being left to weeds and benign neglect. At the end you could peer through a gate of wooden slats in the hope of seeing the coach. Now it has been concreted, the grass cut and the whole place cleaned and tarted up in a manner most unfriendly to ghosts. Behind the wall on the other side of the

Pends, where there is now a museum, stood a house, in the basement of which were some traces of the cathedral buildings. In my youth the Dubs family rented it. Dubs & Co was one of the great locomotive builders in Glasgow. Both the house and the company are now no more.

Before the site of St Leonard's College was taken over by St Leonard's School, part of their buildings, the part which now houses the headmistress, was inhabited by Provost Playfair. He who did so much, rightly or wrongly, to tidy up St Andrews like a canny animal who likes to camouflage itself in discreet surroundings, favoured for his own home a long, low house behind walls rather than the exuberant architecture of the new St Andrews which he encouraged (see once again *Building for a New Age*). Mrs Helen Cook describes the vigorous administrator of both India and St Andrews as 'a man of lively and original mind, of whimsical humour with an interest in mathematics and things mechanical'. It is to Mrs Helen Cook that I am indebted for the account of the garden he created at St Leonard's West. Her account in full can be found in the *Scots Magazine* or, reprinted, in the *St Leonard's School Gazette*, 1990–1. According to Mrs Cook, the provost designed his garden to 'intrigue, entertain, educate and even to startle'. In it stood vases and fountains fed from the mill lade that ran through it. This stream also provided power for many models and a bridge incorporating a crocodile (in stone) bearing the devil which supported a group of Chinese figures. Models of ships also sailed on the stream. The centre-piece of the garden was a pagoda topped by figures of men and beasts that danced in the wind. The pagoda was 90 ft high and must, indeed, have been a striking erection. Whether it was beautiful is another question. In its photograph it looks like an elegant oil rig.

Once again I must remark what an accomplished family the Playfairs were and are. The provost in his photograph is all that one would hope for – a cliff-like brow, domineering nose and humorous mouth. He is wearing a stock and waistcoat, not shown in colour, but clearly of the richest plum with fine embroidery, such as the Tailor of Gloucester would have been proud of. One can see how the strands which gave rise to the science of Lord Playfair, the theology of the Revd Patrick and the *Beggar's Opera* of Sir Nigel are interwoven. The most famous living Playfair, Sir Edward, distinguished in the Civil Service and later in business, wrote me a letter in connection with this book in that excellent simple prose such as is hardly ever met today. It should be held out as an example to all civil servants and schoolteachers. The only failing of this family seems to have been occasionally at golf. Elliot, my friend, was an adventurous golfer but with too long and erratic a swing for the confinement of his shots to the fairway.

As a plaque informs you, Professor Brewster, principal of the university and the inventor of the kaleidoscope, lived in part of the Playfair house. What the plaque does not mention is that according to Lord Cockburn 'no one speaks much of him. With a beautiful taste for science he has a stronger taste for making enemies of friends.' Now all the land between the Pends and the priory wall belongs to St Leonard's School. The pendulum of educational fashion is swinging back from mixed education. I am in general against the segregation of the sexes. But for some period (not too long) during adolescence segregation in education seems a good thing. Some girls claim that it gives them self-confidence. There is evidence that in mixed schools there is a bias in favour of the boys (I am slightly surprised to hear this). What was undoubtedly true was that in single-sex institutions many girls, who are naturally more serious than boys, were brought up to believe that good marks were vital to life (a view shaken off by many later on). I used to examine for travelling scholarships. The description by the girls of what they wanted to do was beyond belief. One girl enlightened us as to her reasons for wanting to go to the French Riviera. When we asked what to do she replied, 'To stay in a nunnery and take brass rubbings of the tombs in the churches.' We told her that she could do that in Britain and ordered her to go away and come back with a programme suitable for Nice, Monte Carlo, etc. Judging from their gazette, things are much better at St Leonard's. In the latest gazette there are accounts and pictures of expeditions to Nepal and the wildlife reserves of Africa. The old St Andrews habit of bathing no doubt still continues, but the only slightly more salubrious sport of sailing (and capsizing) has been introduced in the school – and even the building of the boats. As for boarding schools, eight to eighteen, for which time many boys endure them, is certainly too long. But perhaps for some children a spell away from home may be good.

St Leonard's has always had a fair quota of English girls. It, along with the university and the Madras College, is one of the three great teaching establishments of St Andrews. It was founded in 1877 in the building which we passed at the corner of Queens Gardens and Queens Terrace. A pioneer institution in the education of women, its first headmistress was Dame Louisa Lumsden. This in itself was an innovation; most colleges which took women were presided over by men. Dame Louisa Lumsden joined the professors who were her contemporaries by living a very long time. She died in 1935 aged ninety-three. She also achieved the double distinction of being a pioneer of women's education at St Leonard's and the first warden of the first university residence for women in Britain – also in St Andrews. She was, with another St Andrews woman, Miss Cook, one of the first two women to pass the Classical Tripos at Cambridge (the examination of which A.E. Housman remarked, 'The decay of English Classical scholarship can be dated, almost exactly, from the inauguration of the Cambridge

Classical Tripos'). Not only education but other causes throughout the land, such as the suffragettes, the Territorial Army, the RSPCA and those admirable institutions, the Womens Rural Institutes, all owe much to her. The school has maintained a high standard of scholarship – Lord Bryce and Sir Henry Craik were among its early examiners – but equally it has an athletic tradition worthy of Rugby. Each girl had to undergo one period of gymnastic instruction per week. Participation in team games was compulsory. The girls' prowess at cricket was demonstrated on their excellent playing fields behind the abbey wall at the fathers' match, in which such well-known cricketing-golfers as Colonel Skene took part, resplendent in MCC caps (he must, I think, have been an honorary father). Golf and cricket are said not to mix, but Colonel Skene and Colonel Lindsay, who played a straight club up and down as in an off drive, proved that this was not always true. Colonel Skene wielded a putter with a square, wooden head and was a scratch golfer.

In my youth the St Leonard's girls were scattered in houses over the town, including Abbotsford Crescent. They were a familiar sight marching through the town in crocodiles, felt hats bobbing and pig-tails swinging. I regret that they have been corralled by the Pends but I see that it is convenient. Sir Edward Playfair's mother introduced the cloaks which St Leonard's girls wore in winter. Sir Edward writes:

One holiday she had been to Brittany. The Breton peasant women all wore those dark cloaks which are so familiar from French paintings and as is the general rule in peasant societies children wore the same only smaller. My mother's relations bought one for her, and she wore it to St Leonards. At that time there was no uniform. The great Miss Dove [the headmistress] said, 'Harriet Leighton, come over here and let me see your cloak.' She looked at it carefully and said, 'I think that is just what we need for a school uniform.'

While we look round with pleasure at St Leonard's Chapel and the back of Queen Mary's House, we should remember one of the greatest benefactors of St Andrews, the Marquis of Bute, who when rector of the university spent a great deal of money and energy on restoring the neglected relics of St Andrews' splendour. We are indebted to him more than anyone else, not only for rescuing such of the medieval buildings as survive but for teaching that our inheritance is worth preserving.

The precincts of the priory and St Leonard's College seem a good place to end an examination of the city. St Andrews is a small place. Its layout has not greatly changed. Looking at early prints of the city you can clearly trace it as it is today. The first pictures of golfers show the bridge over the Swilcan burn. An oil painting that I possess painted by Paterson about 100 years ago shows the view from the harbour much as it still is – though the women on the pier are dressed in white mutches, rather Dutch in style. Since St Andrews has been troubled by neither industry nor oil and golf is spreading west, there is no reason why the eastern streets should not for many years retain their beauty and their (comparative) tranquillity.

Nevertheless, you must not look on St Andrews as a museum, preserved only for tourists and golfers. It is a town of vitality whose beauty changes with the years, the seasons and, indeed, every day with the weather and light. If the well-kept Victorian terraces with their washed steps and polished bell pulls, salient memories of St Andrews' houses in my childhood, seem unremarkable and perhaps austere, they are also human and serviceable and I am sure people still find them so. Other cities may surpass St Andrews as places to visit and admire, but I wonder if they are better places in which to live?

Bibliography

All books mentioned in Acknowledgements, plus:

Cant, Dr R.G., *The University of St Andrews*, Scottish Academic Press, Edinburgh, 1970.

Clark, Alwyn, *Queen Mary's House*, Council of St Leonard's School, 1977.

Cockburn, Lord, *Circuit Journeys*, Byways, Hawick, 1983.

Everard, H.S.C., *A History of the Royal and Ancient Golf Club, St Andrews 1754–1900*, Edinburgh, William Blackwood, 1907.

Fergusson, Sir J., (ed.), *George Dempster's Letters to Sir Adam Fergusson*, Macmillan, 1934.

Frew, Dr John, (ed.), *Building for a New Age*, Crawford Centre for the Arts, 1984.

Lamont-Brown, R., *The Life and Times of St Andrews*, John Donald, Edinburgh, 1989.

Lang, Andrew, *St Andrews*, Longman, London, 1893.

Lewis, Gifford, *The Selected Letters of Somerville and Ross*, Faber & Faber, London, 1989.

Macaulay, J.S.A., (ed.), *St Leonard's School 1877–1977*, St Leonards School and Blackie, 1977.

MacDonald, Prof J.A., *Trees in St Andrews*, St Andrews Preservation Trust, 1977.

Pearson, J.M., *A Guided Walk Round St Andrews*, printed by Rutherford, Broughty Ferry, 1990.

Read, Prof J., *Historic St Andrews and its University*, W.C. Henderson, St Andrews, 1955.

Reid, Wemyss, *Memoirs and Correspondence of Lyon Playfair*, Cassell, London, 1899.

Rogers, C., *History of St Andrews with a full account of recent improvements in the city*, Edinburgh, 1849.

St Andrews Preservation Trust, *Three Decades of Historial Notes*, 1991.

First Statistical Account of St Andrews and St Leonards 1793, reprinted by the University of St Andrews, 1989.

Second Statistical Account of St Andrews and St Leonards 1838, reprinted by the University of St Andrews, 1989.

Index